THE UTOPIA OF WORLD COMMUNITY

The Utopia of
World Community

An Interpretation of the World Council
of Churches for Outsiders

A. J. VAN DER BENT

SCM PRESS LTD

334 01724 6

First published 1973
by SCM Press Ltd
56 Bloomsbury Street, London

© SCM Press Ltd 1973

Printed in Great Britain by
Northumberland Press Limited
Gateshead

CONTENTS

Preface   vii

I Quests for World Community   1

   World Movements and World Organizations   1
   World Brotherhood   4
   Baha'ism   8
   Islam   10
   Judaism   13
   Buddhism and Hinduism   15
   The United Nations   16
   Communism   17

II The World Council of Churches   23

   Nature and Constitution   23
   Organization and Function   27
   Programmes and Activities   30
   A New Structure   38
   Relations with Other Ecumenical Bodies   40
   Relations with the Roman Catholic Church   41

III Justice and Service   44

   The Commission on the Churches' Participation in
      Development   45
   The Programme to Combat Racism   51
   The Commission of the Churches on International Affairs   55
   Inter-church Aid, Refugee and World Service   59
   The Christian Medical Commission   63

IV A Summary of Criticisms   66

   The Conservative Critique   66
   The Passionate Argument for Reunion   68
   The 'Death of Confessionalism' Issue   71
   The 'Establishment' Issue   74
   The 'Third World' Issue   77
   The Clergy versus Laity Argument   79
   The 'Grass-Roots' Issue   81
   The 'Third Ecumenical Movement' Argument   83
   The Need for Deeper Sociological Analysis   85

V   The Dialogue with People of Living Faiths   90

     Before and after Uppsala, 1968   92
     Orthodox Contributions   96
     'The Precarious Vision'   98

VI   '... and Ideologies'   103

     The Christian Aversion to Atheism   103
     The World Council and the Problem of Ideology   106
     Christianity is not an Ideology   111
     Ideology in a Constructive Context   115

VII The Humanness and Identity of the Institution   121

     'Sacred Literature'   124
     Salt and Leaven   128
     The Disunity of the Church   132

VIII The Promise of a World Community   139

     Organization of the World Council of Churches
       (Diagram)   148
     For Further Reading   149

PREFACE

The emphasis in the sub-title of this book is on the word 'outsiders'. Many books on the twentieth-century ecumenical movement and on the World Council of Churches have been written for 'insiders', that is to say, for committed ecumenical Christians who know what the word 'ecumenical' stands for and who have been in contact with the World Council in one way or another. The 'outsiders' I have in mind include 'marginal' Christians who frequently confuse the adjective 'ecumenical' with the adjective 'economical', and have no knowledge of the history of the World Council of Churches. Perhaps they just know that there is some kind of international Christian establishment in Geneva, Switzerland, and are not even sure about that. In addition, I am writing for 'better informed' Christians who do not speak much about the World Council except in terms of a Christian bureaucracy and an isolated establishment which has ceased to be a driving force for the 'real' ecumenical movement. Speaking of outsiders, I would certainly wish also to include 'people of other living faiths' and 'adherents of a secular ideology', to use the ecumenical jargon, for whom two chapters have specially been written on the Council's concern for dialogue.

Can an insider write intelligently and understandably for an outsider? Does his presentation and interpretation of an international Christian organization, for which he works and to whose task he is devoted, not turn out to be a clever defence of that organization? Or, on the contrary, are his criticisms so negative and severe that he perhaps pleases the reader but misrepresents and misinterprets the World Council? I find it difficult to give satisfying answers to these questions. The reader has to judge for himself. I can only assure him that I have no desire to praise or blame the World Council of

Churches. I have tried to look with him as an outsider at the
Ecumenical Centre in Geneva. As Librarian of the World
Council I am in the privileged position of being in contact with
a great number of different people. Through them I have
learned increasingly that a true insider must remain to some
degree a curious outsider, as far as that is possible. One can
never be sure, however, whether one is engaged in an effective
dialogue between insider and outsider. I hope, of course, that
some insiders, too, will read this book and hear the challenging
voice of some outsiders. Unfortunately, only a minority of
ecumenical Christians really want to know how others look
at the movement and the Geneva-based international organization.

On several occasions it has been pointed out to me that there
is hardly any critical literature on the ecumenical movement,
written from a constructive point of view. This is quite true.
The great bulk of material is of an informative, descriptive and
apparently 'objective' nature. The *raison d'être* of the World
Council of Churches is in no way seriously questioned. The
'unpleasant' literature is mainly written from an uninformed,
unfair or sectarian perspective. It is not very difficult to
produce books or articles which contain critique solely for the
sake of critique. Any religious or secular international institution can easily be criticized for its inadequacy, ineffectiveness
or its anachronistic nature.

The reader who wishes to obtain more detailed knowledge
about the World Council of Churches must consult other
books. For his information I have added a short annotated list
of recent works on the World Council as a whole and on some
of its specific activities. The second and third chapters of this
book contain only a brief and selective description of the
various units, sub-units and staff working groups of the Council.
Reference is made to a minimum of the innumerable conferences and documents. I have also mentioned only a few
personal names. My main purpose is to enquire about the
World Council of Churches' creative and concrete contribution to mankind as a whole and its place as a community in the

midst of other religious and secular communities, which together form the present world community.

Examining the World Council from this particular angle,
I have purposely devoted little attention to the Council's concern for unity among the various Christian churches, its duty
to bear Christian witness in the contemporary world and its
investigation of relationships between the church and the
world. Many books describing the nature, aims and functions
of the World Council of Churches within the traditional framework of the three twentieth-century ecumenical movements,
namely Faith and Order, the International Missionary Council
and Life and Work, have by-passed a basic question, namely
how the Council discovers and evaluates itself as *a* community
in equal and reciprocal relations with other communities. The
emphasis has first of all and almost exclusively been laid on
the World Council's task of bringing the churches closer
together so that their message may be heard more widely and
their common service to the world may be more acceptable
and effective.

While these concerns remain real and valid, they reveal
little of the World Council's self-understanding and awareness
that it is only one world family among other world families.
For this very reason I have discussed the Council's humanitarian and service programmes in depth less from its own
standpoint and more from a total world perspective. Summarizing next the various criticisms of the World Council of
Churches, I have attempted to show that most of these
criticisms have some bearing on the life and organization of
the Council itself, but again do not clearly and critically relate
the Council's existence to other contemporary international
organizations and movements. The weaknesses, shortcomings
and failures within the World Council and its constituent
churches are closely examined, but little thought is given to
the Council's possible difficulty in finding its proper place as
one world community among other world communities.

The question then arises whether the World Council as an
international ecclesiastical organization has made some pro-

gress in seeking sincere and meaningful dialogues with other world religious families and entering into conversations with major ideological movements which claim the same allegiance from their followers as all world religions. As the whole matter of dialogue with representatives of world religions and contemporary ideologies is still far from being taken for granted within ecumenical Christianity, I touch finally upon the problem of the World Council's authentic humanness and true humaneness in facing the multi-religious and non-religious world with the status of a *human* institution, seeing that world as made up of *human* groups and communities and not as fields of penetration and action, for the verification of the validity of its own programmes. I believe that this exercise will not weaken or threaten, but purify and enrich the very existence of the World Council of Churches.

I

Quests for World Community

World Movements and World Organizations

More than ever before, men and women of the twentieth century have believed and are still convinced that mankind is on its way towards creating an enduring world community. The human race, it is now claimed, has gained sufficient experience, wisdom and power to realize and to manifest its global unity. The generation before and after World War I spoke boldly of a universal brotherhood, anticipated the total abolition of war and prepared for the reign of international law and order under a world federation of governments. As world history moved on, the League of Nations was replaced by the United Nations and the term 'universal brotherhood' was exchanged for such phrases as 'international co-operation', 'world strategy for peace', 'collective security' and 'global cultural integration'. There is no doubt that this unique world organization still shows some weaknesses and that its prestige and effectiveness would be improved if nations turned to it more consistently, but the great hope still persists that all peoples will come close together, creating the political, socioeconomic and spiritual climate for a growing world civilization.

The twentieth century is also the era of the ecumenical movement. The Christian churches in six continents have finally come to the conclusion that only a world-wide and re-united church can proclaim an authentic gospel and work side by side with the world towards the common goal of greater unity and well-being among all men. Although Christians still

find it very difficult to define the relationship between the
unity of the church and the unity of the world, they now
more or less agree that the manifestation of the unity of all
Christians cannot be envisaged apart from the promotion of
the unity of mankind. This year the World Council of
Churches, deeply committed to the task of a twofold unifica-
tion, is celebrating its twenty-fifth anniversary. Over the last
few decades Judaism has also created its own international
organizations such as the World Jewish Congress and the
World Conference of Jewish Organizations, in order to foster
the unity of the Jewish people and to assist the development
of Jewish social and cultural life throughout the world. B'nai
B'rith, the oldest and largest Jewish service organization, has
spread in various continents and continues its mission of
'uniting persons of the Jewish faith in the work of promoting
their highest interests and those of humanity'.

Islam has made great progress in Africa, Asia and beyond
these continents, proclaiming God's sovereignty over the
whole universe. Its ultimate ideal of world community is
expressed in the vision of a confederation of autonomous
states, associated together for upholding freedom of conscience and for the maintenance of peace and co-operation in
promoting human welfare throughout the world. Islam, now
counting almost 500 million followers, claims to have laid the
foundations of true universal brotherhood, excluding all discrimination and privilege based on colour, race, nationality,
status or wealth. After World War II, Asian Buddhism planned
seriously for a world mission. This world religion now has
a total estimated membership of 180 million, and there can be
little doubt that it will continue to attract a wider allegiance.
The World Fellowship of Buddhists was founded in 1950. The
great Sixth Council which was held in Rangoon from 1954 to
1956, to celebrate the 2500th anniversary of the Buddha's
birth, became a symbol of world-wide Buddhist unity. Buddhism has given new evidence of its transcendent universalism
and its capacity to cut through traditional forms of beliefs and
hopes with innovating spiritual power. Hinduism, too, count-

ing close to 450 million disciples, has increasingly turned
towards missionary endeavour. Its genius is its ability to absorb
and to comprehend. Hinduism can offer to the world a unique
synthesis, shaped through thousands of years of history, paving
the way for religious reunion between East and West.

Finally, various ideologies, particularly some 'world-revolutionary' ideologies, have had a great bearing on the evolution
of this century. Political scientists and sociologists frequently
class not only democratic movements and attitudes such as
pacific democracy, economic liberalism and internationalism
under the heading 'pragmatic' ideology, but also religious
movements and churches (Islam, Christianity). In speaking of
'world-revolutionary' ideologies, we have first of all Marxism-
Leninism, or in more general terms communist ideology, in
mind. According to Marxist doctrine, the classless society to be
established through the solidarity and the world-wide struggle
of the proletariat of all countries will do away with alienation,
exploitation and war, merging nations in one socialist brotherhood. Although communist ideology has been wavering and
unclear about the 'strategy' to be used for the attainment of
this goal, it remains the most powerful ideology of this century, inspiring and uniting millions of people in their efforts to
build a more just, equal and international society.

Deliberately and not accidentally speaking in the same
breath of various contemporary political, ideological and
religious movements and international organizations, we
immediately face a host of complicated questions. Do all these
movements and world-wide organizations really anticipate a
spiritual, political and cultural progress in this century and the
next? Are all indeed promoting international peace, human
welfare and global justice? Can each faith, each international
political organization and each world ideology contribute
equally and at the same time to the quest for a world
community? Are they not, on the contrary, competing with
one another and diminishing precious chances for open dialogue, deeper understanding and mutual correction? Does the
search for greater 'internal' unity within each religion and

the desire to express this unity in an adequate form automatically and necessarily include a contribution to the unity of
mankind? Is it desirable that world religions and their 'ecumenical' organs should play any part in world affairs? Are not
humanitarian movements and secular ideologies better equipped to deal with the many problems of enhancing a world
community without the interference of world religions? Or
are not, on the other hand, international political organizations
and ideological movements in danger of weakening their cause
by becoming pseudo-religions and claiming total allegiance?
Can we speak of a world-wide unity at different levels, and if
so, how are these levels related to one another?

Looking for a moment more critically and in greater detail
at the programmes of various world movements and the
activities of internal bodies which I have mentioned, we should
try to keep these questions constantly in mind in order to discover whether the quest for world community and the pursuit
of universal unity are indeed genuine and based on a solid foundation. The following short survey will also help us to interpret, I hope without too much bias, the nature, aims and
functions of the World Council of Churches in the light of
further questions and findings.

World Brotherhood

In the year 1919, just ten months after the end of the
disaster of World War I, delegates from twenty nations,
assembled in the First World-Brotherhood Congress in London,
proclaimed: 'The nineteenth century made the world a neighbourhood. It is the task of the twentieth century to make the
world a brotherhood. If men are to live together at all on this
crowded earth, it is necessary that all human relations be
adjusted on the basis of justice and brotherhood.'

Certainly, the solemn assembly emphasized that the creation
of an authentic world community will involve some thorough-
going changes in the ideas of men and the organization of
society. Nations must learn to think of other peoples as
brothers and respect the contribution and life of each people.

Only a cultivation and growth of an international mind will lead men of every race to love and trust all others. Universal brotherhood implies that 'industry must become a social service and the whole process of industry, both in production and distribution, must represent the co-operation of all in behalf of all'. But the London brotherhood message also confidently affirmed : 'Humanity has struck its tents and once more is on the march. The hour is freighted with splendid opportunity. Men are growing a great new passion for justice and brotherhood. It is possible now for humanity to advance a thousand years towards the Kingdom of God.'

Brotherhood is an old concept. The Stoics had already conceived the idea that mankind is one big family and that all human beings are brothers. They were opposed to slavery and rejected the teaching that a slave is another being than a free-born citizen. Liberal movements in the Christian church have stressed for centuries that Jesus himself preached a gospel of brotherhood. 'You are all brothers ... for you have one Father who is in heaven' (Matt. 23.8f.). The Enlightenment, combining the Stoic teachings and a generous Christian message of brotherly tolerance and love, developed the thesis that each man is born with the same human dignity and rights, which constitute the basis of the fellowship of mankind. The French Revolution finally incorporated the concept of brotherhood (*fraternité*) in a new state legislation. The term was widely used as an official motto in the democratic ideology of the Second French Republic.

The new element in the flood of twentieth-century books and conference reports is the emphasis on the *final realization* of the ideal on a world scale. Now the time has come when 'our children will be brought up in a spirit of universal brotherhood, and our grandchildren will live in a society of universal brotherhood'. The task before mankind is clear and simple. Close, active contact and co-operation with all bodies and individuals interested in the brotherhood of men have to be established. An active part should be taken in making universal brotherhood a basis for the education of all children. The idea of world brotherhood in the life and thought of men must be ardently promoted all over the world. There can be no doubt that this century will at last create a world at peace, under common law and order, united in one brotherhood of the human race. This new world will be mindful of the superficial character of most differences, and of the wisdom of being ready to arbitrate them in the spirit of good will and good faith. It should be noted that the United Nations' Declaration of the Rights of the Child later included the phrase : 'The child shall be brought up in a spirit of universal brotherhood.'

World religions like Christianity, Judaism, Islam and Buddhism did not join the chorus of international brotherhood except for individual followers in one or another religion. More recent religious encyclopedias, theological handbooks and social science dictionaries have dropped the word 'brotherhood' entirely. Any definition of the term is abstract and senseless. Precisely what bonds bind the human race together remains an open question. Is it man's blood, his reason or his faith? How reasonable has man been in the course of history? Do all men share in the same faith? When we cannot clearly answer these questions, a world brotherhood will not come into being simply by declaring the need for it.

It is not true, as our pious and benevolent fathers believed, that present proximity ensures unity. The farther peoples still live apart, the friendlier they are and the more they seem to esteem and to tolerate each other. As the crowding together in this world becomes increasingly severe, men easily develop a strong distrust and an intense dislike for each other. Furthermore, it is not true that a common interest in peace and brotherhood is a sufficient base to hold men together. Not that common interests are of secondary importance; indeed they bind men together up to a certain point. But as soon as that point is reached, competing interests will be manifested from each side. Men are basically still separated, and speak of international community only out of a particular interest. Moreover, communication and education remain an uncertain foundation for unity. The spreading of information about different

peoples can be not only a means of bringing them closer together but also a means of keeping them separated. Believers in
brotherhood fail to recognize that just because they know
more about peoples they like, it does not follow that they
really like the peoples about whom they know more. Even
human similarities, such as common physical and emotional
structures, do not constitute a fuller and more secure ground-
ing for human unity. No one can deny these similarities; they
are intrinsic elements of unity. But one can question seriously
whether they are sufficient for human unity and should count
for more than men's differences.

In addition, it is quite naïve to believe that it would be
sufficient to embody the moral imperative of brotherhood in
a universally accepted law. It is also naïve to think that mankind lacks an international government only because no one
has conceived a proper blueprint for it. No wonder that the
advocates of brotherhood have a touching faith in the power of
a formula over the real unfolding of human history.

In all the brotherhood literature of this century, there is a
denial of the fact that the transition from a particular to a
universal community is a far more complicated process than
men can anticipate. It is not just a process moving at a
different rate from those which produced larger and larger
communities in the history of mankind. It is in fact a process
so completely different in kind that we hardly know whether
it can be initiated within the limits of history. If it is within
men's power and possibility, only desperate historical necessity will make it so. Major world religions, therefore, cannot
be enthusiastic about universal brotherhood, as they remember
too well what men have accomplished and still can accomplish
in the way of madness, lies and destruction – and all this not
by means of their instincts, but by means of their very reason
and faith which supposedly bind all men together in one
common fellowship. Every 'reasonable' man should admit that
other epochs of tragic history will be required to achieve that
world brotherhood which is so impossible and yet so necessary
to establish.

Finally, the assertion that the New Testament gospel is in fact a simple message of brotherhood rests upon a random selection and a deceiving interpretation of a single text. The word 'brother' is used in the New Testament only for those who are baptized members of the Christian church. The intimate relationship between fellow Christians cannot be better expressed than by the word 'brother'. According to Hebrews 2.11, Jesus himself is not ashamed of calling his disciples brothers. But the Bible is too realistic and too specific to lump all human beings together on the basis of some natural bonds and common characteristics.

Baha'ism

One of the few religions which still has the phrase 'world brotherhood' officially on its banner is Baha'ism. This syncretistic (the word means 'combining different forms of belief or practice') and universalist religion originated in Shiïte Islam, but also closely resembles Unitarianism and Ramakrishnan Hinduism. It aims to establish a unity of the human race and the unity of all religions. There are no chosen people, no superior or inferior races. All humanity is equally sacred and precious in the eyes of God. All faiths – Hindu, Christian, Jewish, Mohammedan, Buddhist and Confucian – are basically the same. Their differences and peculiarities are superficial and due to accidents of climate, geography and economic conditions. There is one great spiritual reality behind them. Philosophically, all religions agree; it is only in their mythology and ritual that they have developed differences.

The Baha'i religion further preaches the abandonment of all discrimination based on class, cultural, national, racial or religious distinctions, equal rights for the sexes, a universal compulsory programme of education, a simultaneous universal programme of disarmament, a universal supplementary language to be used as a means of international communication and the establishment of an international tribunal.

By his own testament, Baha'Ullah, the founder of the religion, named his oldest grandson, Shoghi Effendi, as 'Guardian of the Cause of God' and as his successor. From 1923 on, Effendi made his home in Haifa, Israel, thereafter the principal centre of Baha'ism. It is difficult to accept both that this out-spoken universalist faith is at the mercy of a hereditary apos-tolic succession and that it is to be watched over from one major spiritual centre. The bulk of Baha'i publications appear to come from one family, namely Baha'Ullah, his son Abdul Baha and from Shoghi Effendi. Although Baha'i temples were erected in several countries and Baha'i centres claim a con-siderable number of disciples, the total membership is not revealed. Baha'ism cannot be classed among the world religions.

Serious reservations about the Baha'i religion, however, do not entirely rule out the present need and the real opportunity for a World Parliament of Religions addressing itself to divided mankind. Religion has been a divisive force in history for far too long. Even in this century, countries have been split apart by religious divisions. The time has come for all religions to cease explaining their basic differences and to recognize their common beliefs and their common purposes for the good of mankind. The demand that religious men should work together for justice, understanding and peace is an urgent imperative from which no religion can turn away. Yet, the combining of common forces and resources for the sake of fostering greater justice, understanding and peace can only be based on a 'temporary unity' of religions which is an uncertain and weak unity, and lasts as long as the common beliefs are not questioned and corrected anew by an ultimate faith which several religions would not accept as the right interpretation of their heritage. Moreover, the unity among religions remains a narrow kind of unity because only religious men, and not all human beings, are included in this unity. Precisely because religions can make some allowances and concede a num-ber of common denominators (how many common denomin-ators?), they are in danger of seemingly combining their forces and defending themselves against a growing sec-ular world civilization. True unity is still something other than the unity of religious convictions and practices.

Islam

In the course of its history, Islam (Arabic, meaning 'submission' to the will of God) has spread over three continents, from West Africa to the Indonesian archipelago. The greater part of Muslim missionary activity in the past has been by way of vigorous individual effort. At the turn of this century, organized effort for the propagation of Islam was undertaken by various missionary agencies and movements. Islam is making headway in Europe and North America. It is not difficult to explain the reason for its steady growth. It has the strength of an evangelical creed, a noble simplicity, an obvious piety. Its faith in one God makes its central teaching a clearly intelligible one.

The Qur'ān stresses the unity of mankind, emphasizing that man has been created of one kind. The whole of God's creation is in harmony. There is no discord, disorder or incongruity. The human race can fulfil the purpose for which it was created. Any disorder or maladjustment that may be observed results from misuse or contravention of the divine laws governing the universe. Men are destined to achieve a universal brotherhood. Because of this central doctrine Islam does not carry the stigma of colonialism. Its sense of the brotherhood of all believers contrasts in the mind of the Third World with the inequalities imposed by white rule, often identified with Christianity. For this very reason Islam remains a simple, burning faith which can reawaken the dignity of all peoples who are in danger of losing their identity through foreign domination. Islam can claim to have laid the foundations for an ever-growing unity of mankind and to be in the forefront of the battle against the divisive and destructive powers of this world.

Curiously enough, a serious contradiction between religious theory and secular practice is reflected in the history of the Caliphate, which manifested the unity of all Muslim peoples and strengthened their Islamic ecumenical consciousness. According to the rules laid down by the theologians after

Mohammed's death, the Caliphate had to take over the role of the Prophet in government, jurisdiction and all other public affairs. In pursuit of this idea, the Islamic state instituted a single citizenship entailing overall allegiance to a single head of state, the Calipha (meaning vicegerent or successor), who was the guardian of the Pax Islamica and responsible for the welfare of all sections of the population inspired and united by common ideals. The office of Calipha was elective or, as happened in the case of Umar, the Calipha was nominated by his predecessor and approved by his people. The Calipha held office for life and devoted his whole time and all his faculties to the service of the commonwealth, bound by the ordinances of divine law and by the principles on which they were based. Because of many political antagonisms and hereditary problems, the Caliphate gradually lost its power until it was no more than a puppet in the hands of rival governments. Soon after the end of the fourteenth century it was supplanted by the Turkish Sultanate, so that even the Arab prerogatives of the Caliphate no longer remained intact. The abolition of the Caliphate by the Turkish National Assembly in 1924 caused great perturbation among Muslims. However an international Caliphate congress held at Cairo in 1926 decided that until all the Islamic peoples could join in establishing a new Caliphate, the office should remain in abeyance. Moreover, the Caliphate movements in India and Pakistan virtually died out.

After World War II Islam received a certain impetus when India, Pakistan and Indonesia rose to independent status. The sudden realization of their influence in international councils induced the Muslim states to co-ordinate their activities. International conferences in Karachi in 1952 and in Mecca in 1954 resulted in the establishment of a permanent council for organizing meetings to co-ordinate activities for the emancipation of Muslim countries and for raising the cultural, social and economic standards of Muslim people. All Muslim states were, however, aware that it was not possible to revive either the traditional Islamic ideal of unity or the religious approach to foreign affairs, because circumstances were not favourable

to the involvement of religion in the context of relations between nations.

Besides the Caliphate, Islam also instituted a compulsory
pilgrimage for all its followers to Mecca. From the ends of the
earth believers are drawn to the holy city. For every Muslim
the pilgrimage is a deeply emotional and religious experience.
The sacredness of the Ka'bah makes Mecca and its environs a
place of godly peace and refuge. According to the Qur'ān, the
Ka'bah was the first house that was founded for mankind. It is
'the navel of the earth', the mother of all cities. Muslim tradition transferred from Jerusalem the Jewish legends that Mel-
chizedek had set up his altar there and that Abraham had
brought his sacrifice. God commanded Moses to regard the
rock as the place for prayer. The Prophet, finally, abolished
the worship of many idols, installed in the course of time in the
Sacred House, and restored the worship of the One True God.
Although the pilgrimage has since become one of the obliga-
tions incumbent upon every Muslim adult who can afford the
journey, the symbolic significance of Mecca as the truly representative place of an ecumenical gathering of the whole
Islamic world has been insufficiently valued. The dream of a
World Assembly of Islam joined together in spiritual association for the glorification of God and the promotion of world
unity and human welfare has not been realized. In fact, the
tension between the nationalism of various Islamic states and
the Islamic consciousness of international solidarity has been
greatly increased.

Time is not ripe yet, it seems, for a more radical self-examination on the part of Islam. The historical facts of this century
are nevertheless self-evident. The value and feasibility of an
all-embracing religious and social system must be seriously
questioned. While the ideal of the *Corpus Christianum* has
been given up as unrealizable in history, the ideal of the *Corpus
Islamicum* cannot remain unchallenged. Islam, however, still
insists that a theocracy, a total control and domination of the
divine revelation over all realms of human life, can be established. By exchanging the idea of the 'kingdom of God' for the

idea of the 'kingdom of this world', Islam cannot but continue to subscribe to the strategy of 'holy war', believing that Islam can never politically be defeated. The whole world, eschatologically speaking, must and will be subdued and won over to the Islamic faith. Unbelievers will be destroyed. Muslims themselves must answer the questions whether Islam is capable of responding to the unprecedented challenge of Western atheism, secularization and separation of church and state, and whether the Qur'ān as eternally valid and unalterable holy writ can give guidance for future world crises.

Judaism

The eleventh chapter of the book of Genesis tells the story of a 'single people with a single language' building the tower of Babel. God came down to see the tower and 'scattered the sons of man over the whole face of the earth'. The very next chapter records the story of Abraham's calling. He is led by God through the chaotic world of many peoples and races to the centre of a new mankind – the land of Canaan. Henceforth the nations will only be blessed by this one man and this one people, Israel. All the nations of the world will be united again into one people by this one nation. It is wrong to regard Israel's 'particularism' as something set over against its 'universalism', or even opposed to it. In God's plan of salvation Israel will fulfil its 'particular' calling and function only in the context of and for the sake of a universal purpose. Israel's special role lasts from the scattering of mankind in Babel to mankind's being gathered in again in Zion. It performs the representative role of being the one people which mankind originally was. Its particularism as a people has nothing to do with a nationalistic self-consciousness and self-defence. It results from its spiritual calling: to win the nations back to God by communicating the Torah to them.

Over and over again, according to the Jewish scriptures, Israel refused or failed to be faithful to its function and calling. It worshipped other gods and was concerned with its own well-being and security. Consequently it almost took the

place of Babel and represented all mankind in unity and disper-
sion, in pride and sin and fall. God's judgment on his people is
his judgment on all the earth. Israel is scattered among the
nations. But the great prophets speak of an ultimate hope : a
'remnant' of Israel will return and be gathered again, and this
remnant is the *pars pro toto* of mankind. As the house of David
has become a useless instrument, God will grow a new shoot
from the amputated trunk of Jesse. Second Isaiah has a glimpse
of the depth of God's design of salvation : mankind can be
re-united only by the 'suffering servant' who will exterminate
all its guilt. Only through his quiet suffering and his reconciling
death will the kingdom of God be established.

Jerusalem was destroyed by the Romans in AD 70 and the
new state of Israel was created in 1948. Ever since the fall of
Jerusalem in 586 BC the Jews have had to endure centuries of
persecution and ostracism in the many countries in which they
have found themselves, culminating in the Nazi attempt at
genocide. It is extraordinary that they have survived and that
their religion has continued to nourish their dispersed community. The Zionist dream has now been given impressive
substance : a new Jewish nation exists with all the marks of
sovereignty, prosperity and technological might. Though the
majority of Jews still live outside the small country of Israel,
the very existence of a new homeland has strengthened
the self-identity of all Jewish people, whether orthodox or
liberal.

No Jew can or will claim that the present state of Israel is
the eschatological fulfilment of the Bible's promise for Zion.
But what precisely does it represent, not in an ideological but
in a religious sense ? Is there any connection between the
visions of a remnant and a suffering servant and a nation which
can be proud of the industry of its settlers and call on a wealth
of talent ? Is the pugnacity with which it defends its territorial
integrity related to its particular calling as a people to respond
fully to the demands of the Torah ? Are not new gods worshipped again, new measures taken to ensure its comfortable
subsistence ? Only the Jew himself can answer these delicate

questions. His very obedience to God and his service to mankind are at stake.

Buddhism and Hinduism

Christianity, Judaism and Islam are frequently grouped together because of their outspoken monotheism. But other major common characteristics are their faith in God who deals with human history and their anticipation of a kingdom of God embracing mankind in a transcendental (meaning: beyond the natural or rational) harmony and unity. A religious philosophy of history is a typical 'Western' phenomenon. Asian religions like Buddhism and Hinduism have a fundamentally different orientation towards world history. Historical existence, according to them, has no meaning in itself. Man must live in it and act reasonably, but history itself can neither create the new nor be truly real. This implies that there is no awareness of historical time and of a goal towards which the historical process develops. History has no aim, either in time or in eternity. The emphasis is on the individual, and particularly on the comparatively few illuminated who are aware of the human predicament. Man must transcend the ambiguities of life and live within them as someone who has already returned to the Ultimate One. A symbol analogous to that of the kingdom of God does not exist in either religion.

The illusory nature of the phenomenal world requires another symbol, that of reincarnation. Life is a continuous cycle. Man's eternal soul as an immortal entity is on death divested of the human sense-organs and reborn in another body until it may achieve liberation. The individual is essentially constituted by his empirical ego which has to be transmigrated. Once individuality has been overcome, through self-realization, the process of rebirth ceases. Thus there is a continuum and a circulation between all forms of life.

In spite of their a-historical orientation, Hinduism and Buddhism can make their specific contribution to our search for a world community of mankind. Precisely because they are too other-worldly and too mystic to give historic potency to universal ideals, they increasingly inspire disillusioned and tired men of the West by pointing to the meaning of life above and beyond the limits of any particular community. In the light of the shortcomings of Western religions, the validity of the Buddhist or Hindu scheme of salvation may become more self-evident. Buddhism in particular also reveals a profound compassion for the universality of suffering under all dimensions of life. This precious element is often lacking in the Western world because of its historical interpretations of history. A 'kingdom of God' theology has too frequently been overshadowed by manifestations of religious superiority and cultural expansion which have rendered the offer of a growing world community suspicious and unacceptable.

The United Nations

The story of the UN is well-known and does not need to be rehearsed. No one can deny that this first major world organization is still the world's best political hope for substituting the conference table for the battlefield, and for mobilizing the world's resources for the service of humanity. Yet no one can deny either that the UN is still marked by serious weaknesses and limits. Its international actions are still infected by tensions between existing national power structures, and its programmes and purposes often lack any enthusiastic support from governments and populations.

Nationalism as a divisive allegiance towards nation states remains the greatest enemy of internationalism. Expressed in isolationism, it refuses to accept responsibility for other peoples. Nationalism as imperialism seeks national domination over other peoples. One of its important manifestations is in economic nationalism, or the pursuit of policies supporting the selfish economic interests of a country. Nationalism as a religious creed nourishes racism and messianism. In its political, economic or religious forms, this attitude of preferential support continues to create conflicts between nations and prevents the proper functioning of the UN. Nationalism, once a unifying factor in the Western hemisphere and still to a degree necessary for new developing societies in the Third World, may become a disintegrating element in the larger society. Only a tempered form of nationalism may still make a contribution in the context of generous support of the legitimate interests of all nations.

All the activities of the UN will scarcely add up to any sort of world government in the foreseeable future. Regardless of whether such a goal should be deemed to be politically desirable, its likelihood would appear to be too remote to affect the basic patterns of present international co-operation. Even under a world state, while administration would become either 'unitary' or 'federal' in the legal sense, it would still remain multicultural in its composition, creating new problems of supranational and intercultural adjustments.

Communism

Of all recent ideologies, that of communism has had the most profound bearing on world affairs. Communist ideology goes back to Karl Marx, although original Marxism had little to contribute to a theory of international relations. It only stated that class societies and not nations produce conflicts and wars, that the exploited are sacrificed by their exploiters, and that the world proletariat in an international struggle will do away with war, uniting peoples in a global socialist community. Although this ideal, as an expectation, was shared by all inheritors of Marxist doctrine, communism has been unsuccessful in creating universal political ties and establishing lasting supranational relationships. For our purpose it is interesting and revealing to refer briefly to the ill-fated history of the five 'Internationals'.

The First International (Working Men's Association), founded in 1862, officially dissolved itself in Philadelphia in 1876. Both Marx and Engels played a dominant role in several public meetings, but the inner struggle due to the expulsion of Bakunin left the international association lifeless. The Second International, created in 1888 in London, passed into oblivion after January 1915. Again anarchists raised their heads, bringing memories of the split of the First International over Marx and Bakunin. From 1900 onwards the major question was what to do if a world war should break out. The trend was wholly towards revisionism, with Kautsky as its spokesman later. Lenin contemptuously called the Second International a 'letter-box'.

The Third Communist International (Comintern) was founded in Moscow in 1919, and guided by Lenin himself. Its optimistic aim was to replace capitalism by communism all over the world. From Lenin's axiom that imperialism is the inevitable expression of monopoly capitalism, it follows by logical deduction that communist countries are in principle all brothers, for ever united in the struggle against imperialism. Conflicts between communist nations are inconceivable, since all real conflicts are due to catastrophic economic causes, which will disappear with the disintegration of capitalism. Lenin was convinced that the fellowship of all communists is assured when each communist party keeps close relations in matters of doctrine and political alignment with the leading party in Moscow. For almost three decades Stalin adhered to Lenin's principle of monolithic unity, holding a tight monopoly on the manifold operations of the global communist movement. His national policy was considered to be the model of international communism, with the exception of Marshal Tito's Yugoslavia. Under Stalin's guidance the Comintern was dissolved, however, in 1943, as a gesture of unity between Russia and the Western Allies in World War II. Trotsky's Fourth International never succeeded in wielding any power or influence. It lapsed into decay immediately after his death in 1940. The Cominform was organized by Stalin in 1947 and included, besides the USSR, the socialist countries in the East and the communist parties of France and Italy. It was unofficially dissolved after Stalin's death. The monolithic stage of world communism had come to an end, and many changes and struggles within the communist bloc inaugurated a polycentric period of international communism.

Particularly after 1960, numerous contending voices were raised in the communist world, voices of criticism and disagreement seriously weakening the ideological and political unity of the communist bloc. No single leader or single party controls the international scene any longer. The present communist international could be best described as a loosely organized association with broadly defined common objectives. Mutual ideological non-aggression is preferred to a search for precise doctrinal unity. The hope for future majority decisions has been abandoned, and the plan to call a world conference has been indefinitely postponed. Moscow itself has begun to recognize the independence and equality of all national communist parties to such an extent that it has in fact ceased to be the headquarters of an embattled army for organizational discipline and world revolution.

The Moscow-Peking rift aggravated the problem of international solidarity and co-operation still further. The Soviets, claiming that their nuclear might could now deter imperialist countries not only from attacking communist ones but also from warring among themselves, pronounced Lenin's doctrine of the inevitability of war outdated by recent developments. Since major war threatens the survival of all, peaceful co-existence and non-violent transition from capitalism to socialism are possible. Class struggle on the international plane continues in the form of ideological and economic competition. The Chinese claim that a 'low risk' policy, emphasizing peaceful co-existence, only threatens to encourage imperialist aggression. Mao Tse-tung's ideology stresses the necessity of violence and internal revolution in under-developed countries, and insists that it is the responsibility of communist nations to assist and aid revolutionary forces all over the world. The Sino-Soviet conflict continues to pull all communist parties and countries into its vortex. So much for the story of communist international 'co-operation'.

This panorama of world movements, major religions, international organizations and their respective quests and struggles for world community has not proved to be very inspiring and helpful. The road to universal unity seems to be barred by many formidable obstacles. The questions which I raised at the beginning of this first chapter still cannot be answered properly. Before I introduce the World Council of Churches, however, I will nevertheless attempt to draw some tentative conclusions from this survey.

(a) Such concepts as 'humanity', 'mankind' and 'world community' do not yet seem to have been scrutinized and defined adequately. No religion or ideology tells us in what sense it is able to regard mankind as a unity. Sometimes the concept of the solidarity of all men is merely used as a slogan or a magic formula. Not much thought is given to the possibility of the relationship between the growing human interdependence and the unity of the human race.

(b) There seems to be little awareness that world community needs to be understood as the community of communities. The dream of a universal cosmopolitan state is in fact a nightmare. The unity of mankind is not a totalitarian unity, an imposed uniformity. In the universal community of communities, each group should find its own identity. No ideology, and at least no 'Western' religion, states clearly that the unity of mankind is a very long and open-ended process of becoming which can in no way be defined with precision today.

(c) There is little evidence that religions are eager to engage in bilateral or multilateral dialogues on a world scale. Each religion claims to offer better solutions to the problems of mankind and insists on the validity of its own exclusive approach to the question of world community. Eventual dialogue between the major religions is threatened by the attempt to reinforce the 'religious world' by looking for a set of religious common denominators and throwing these up as a dam against the waves of the increasingly 'irreligious world'.

(d) Ecumenical organizations are directed mainly, if not exclusively, towards 'internal affairs'. Only the interests of the faithful are defended and promoted; the eventual unity of a religious community is barely conceived as a manifestation, symbol and anticipation of the unity of mankind. Nor is it sufficiently recognized that all human institutions are not always unmixed blessings, no matter how noble the intentions of their founders. Yet a religion like Judaism and an ideology like communism are in need of a truly 'ecumenical movement'.

(e) A humanistic movement for 'universal brotherhood' fails because of vague and insubstantial universal principles. A religion based on particularity and exclusiveness tends to abandon its universal outlook and to obscure its world-wide missionary function for the sake of its own preservation .

(f) A religion which claims direct control over world affairs has no other choice than to proselytize and to crusade. In order to save the world, mankind must be divided into those who are saved and those who are damned. Until the ultimate goal of salvation is reached, a ceaseless 'holy war' of conquest is to be the instrument of the universalization of religion as well as of the expansion of secular control. Equal status or coexistence with other communities cannot be accepted. A world-revolutionary ideology often resembles and competes with such a religion. Only its motives are seemingly non-religious.

(g) 'Western' religions tend to forget, and some ideologies naïvely to ignore that the universal spread of scientific and technological civilization creates new forms of human bondage, degradation and manipulation. As new instruments of production, transport and communication reduce the space-time dimensions of this world to a fraction of their previous size, leading to a much greater interdependence of all national communities, the moral and social consequences from the extension of all technology are not directly faced. The unifying impact of technology and science does not necessarily imply a development towards more just and harmonious societies and communal human relationships at a deeper level.

(h) Dialogues between religions and ideologies have only passed through an initial stage. The road to better understanding is still obstructed by many prejudices and false accusations. Religions have difficulty in admitting that their world outlook is ideologically conditioned, in whatever situation they may find themselves. Revolutionary ideologies assume that society can truly function only on an exclusively secular basis, without

the interference of a religious system. Both religion and ideology tend to ignore that man is as much a *homo religiosus* as a
homo ideologicus, and that the one conditions the other.

In this context of observations and theses, the questions
arise in what sense the ecumenical movement distinguishes
itself from other world religions and from ideological movements, and to what extent the World Council of Churches
differs from other international organizations. Is the Council
better prepared to formulate more precisely the concepts of
'humanity' and 'mankind'? Does the Council understand itself
primarily as a community in the midst of and in the service of
other communities? Has its organization 'built-in mechanisms'
to escape the danger of serving too exclusively the interests and
needs of its faithful? Has it discovered the promise and the
necessity of engaging widely in bilateral and multilateral dialogues with other religions? Is it sufficiently aware of the tension between being a 'peculiar people' and being dispersed and
'losing itself' in the service of mankind according to the very
contents of its faith? Can the Council concede that its very
being and action are conditioned by ideological presuppositions
and perspectives which needlessly weaken its programmes?
Finally, is its search for unity in its own ranks clearly related
to the search for a world community?

We shall return to these questions in the last four chapters
of this book.* Now I must begin to introduce the constitution
and organization, as well as the aims and functions, of the
World Council of Churches. The following chapters will then
deal with contemporary issues and specific activities within
the ecumenical movement. The reader will have to keep in
mind that my description of such a complex organization as
the World Council of Churches is brief, and marked by an
eclectic approach. Numerous sources of detailed historical and
current information are available and should be consulted if
a thorough knowledge of the organization and the movement
is desired.

---

* It will be seen that several of these thorny and delicate questions
cannot be answered very positively.

II

The World Council of Churches

Nature and Constitution

Delegates from nearly 150 churches and from more than 40 nations attended the First Assembly of the World Council of Churches at Amsterdam in August 1948. With great enthusiasm they gave assent to the following words of the Amsterdam Message: 'Here at Amsterdam we have committed ourselves afresh to Him, and have covenanted with one another in constituting this World Council of Churches. We intend to stay together.' More than 250 churches today share in the fellowship of the Council, representing all Eastern and Western traditions with the exception of the Roman Catholic Church.

In the latest statistics for the major world Christian denominations, the Orthodox churches now include approximately 125 million followers, the Lutheran churches 80 million, the Baptists 65 million, the Presbyterian and Reformed churches 56 million, the Methodists 43 million, the Anglican church 42 million and the Congregationalists 6 million faithful. All these churches and some other churches, united during the last 25 years with another denomination, are represented in the Council. Further included are the Brethren, the Disciples, the Mennonites, the Moravians, the Old Catholic churches, the Quakers, the Salvation Army and some large Pentecostal communities. The Roman Catholic Church now totals approximately 590 million baptized members.

The original Basis of the World Council was very simple. It ran as follows: 'The World Council of Churches is a fellowship of churches which accept the Lord Jesus Christ as God and Saviour.' In response to some criticisms that this formal Basis is inadequate, as it does not encompass the full range of the Christian faith, the Third Assembly of the World Council at New Delhi in 1961 adopted an expansion of the Amsterdam Basis by making it read: 'The World Council of Churches is a fellowship of churches which confess the Lord Jesus Christ as God and Saviour according to the Scriptures and therefore seek to fulfil together their common calling to the glory of the one God, Father, Son and Holy Spirit.'

The Constitution makes it perfectly clear that the World Council of Churches is neither a church nor a new super-church nor a substitute for a united church, nor even a federation of churches, least of all the *Una Sancta* itself. It is simply a Council of *Churches*. Upon entering the Council by accepting the Basis, the constituent bodies remain independent of each other and do not surrender their autonomous character in matters of faith and church order. The Council would overstep the limits it has set itself if it judged the sincerity with which each church accepts the Basis. The only criteria of membership are those of autonomy, size, stability and good relationships with other churches. The autonomy of each church was emphasized even more strongly by the Central Committee of the Council, held at Toronto in July 1950, which stated that 'the member churches of the World Council of Churches do not necessarily recognize each other as true, healthy or complete churches, but they consider the relation of other churches to the Council as a question for mutual consideration'. The Basis, therefore, is not a creed or a confession of faith, but a definition of the nature of the Council and a clarification of the limitations to its membership. It declares the starting-point from which the churches proceed in a mutual sharing of conviction and experience and in a common desire to witness to their faith. As such it also determines the road along which the churches in the Council move together towards greater visible unity.

Ever since its founding, the complex and even paradoxical nature of the World Council of Churches has been recognized. Even today, there are self-doubts and tensions which have not been resolved. On the one hand the Council has reiterated several times that the unity of the church in its Lord Jesus Christ is a gift of God and not a final achievement of committed Christians around the world. On the other hand, as the Council does not wish to abolish the various confessions and traditions of the separated churches but accepts them in the conviction that they can enrich the vision of a fuller and deeper unity, at the same time it remains divided in its understanding of the nature of that ultimate unity which is given by God. The discussion continues whether the Council is merely an instrument or, beyond its constitution and organization, a symbol of the unity of the church. There are those who feel that the World Council is still the most appropriate institution in our time for reflecting the diverse and rich heritage of the member churches. It cannot allow that one view of the church will dominate over the others, as deep differences over the nature of the church and its unity still exist. The Council's Assembly and its Central Committee consequently should not have any constitutional authority over its constituent churches. But there are also those within and outside the Council who are pressing towards the goal of the final realization of the *Una Sancta* and who regard the Council as an anticipation of that end. In their view the Council should become something more than a provisional organization; it should prefigure the organic unity of the one universal Christian church. A number of churches, not yet members of the World Council of Churches, regard full doctrinal agreement as a prerequisite of an authentic manifestation of church unity. Some still hold that the search for and expression of visible unity is not the foremost task, because the true unity of the church has an invisible and spiritual character.

The third sentence of the Basis: ... 'and therefore seek to

fulfil together their common calling' also lends itself to different interpretations. What does the Council's common witness and service include and not include? It is obviously the task of the World Council to promote the fellowship of the churches across all geographical, political and ideological boundaries, to provide manifold opportunities for Christians of different backgrounds and convictions to discuss crucial current issues and to enable them to speak with a common voice in matters which concern them, leading to common action as they desire. To this end the Council is commissioned by the churches to call international conferences on specific subjects as occasion may require, and to conduct various studies on inter-confessional and interdisciplinary levels. However, when the World Council's Assembly or any of its various committees publishes a conference report or issues a public statement, it speaks only for itself. The decisions of its committees relate to the Council's programme as such. As a general rule, recommendations and resolutions 'are referred to the churches for study and appropriate action'. The Council 'takes direct action only within the mandate received from its member churches'. In the case of the World Conference on Church and Society, held at Geneva in 1966, the gathering did not even speak on behalf of the World Council, but spoke *to* the Council and its constituent bodies.

The question who is responsible for a service rendered or a common action is further complicated by the question of the nature and aim of such a service or action. The fact that the World Council's staff and its committees are deliberately composed of the widest possible Christian representation of different regions, traditions and intellectual and spiritual points of view, does not necessarily ensure that the Council speaks relevantly to each of the political, social and economic problems of contemporary man. Its Commission on Inter-church Aid, Refugee and World Service, to be sure, has aided victims of several natural and man-made disasters, has cared for the sick, has helped to resettle numerous refugees and assisted various countries in their socio-economic task of nation-building, without reference to the race, creed or political views of the recipients. But were these programmes conceived of and carried out with the sole purpose of contributing to the building up of a world community of communities? Was it not in some way necessary to ease the churches' conscience and to compensate for the slow progress in matters of church unity by manifesting at least a common front in charitable and humanitarian service? Similarly, the Commission of the Churches on International Affairs and the Department on Church and Society have at various times advanced proposals and statements on such issues as disarmament, the cessation of nuclear weapons testing, refugees, religious liberty, human rights, fair trade agreements, national self-determination and economic assistance to developing countries which were favourably received by international organizations, governments and heads of state. Nevertheless, the question can and should be asked again whether these pronouncements served in part to strengthen the Council's very existence and to emphasize its continuous relevance in world affairs. Since the activities of the Commission of the Churches on International Affairs, the Programme to Combat Racism and the Commission on the Churches' Participation in Development are not automatically the consequence of theological and missionary reflections, the Council's engagement in the renewal of society could be considered an inconclusive step beyond its own present internal condition. It should also be kept in mind that some member churches are critical of the Council's seemingly too progressive stand and wish to return to unresolved matters 'at home'. These delicate problems will be discussed further in the latter part of this book.

Organization and Function

The organizational structure of the World Council of Churches, in contrast with, say, the hierarchical structure of the Roman Catholic Church, can be visualized as a pyramid turned upside-down on its tip. The member churches themselves, as indicated before, are the supreme authority, and exercise control over the Council. To this end the constituency of the World Council is represented by approximately 750 delegates to the Assembly, which meets every six or seven years to establish the broad outlines of the Council's basic policy. The Assembly elects from its membership a six-member praesidium and the members of a Central Committee.

The Central Committee is the interim policy-making body which originally consisted of 90 members; at the New Delhi Assembly the number was raised to 100, at the Uppsala Assembly to 120. It carries out 'the Assembly's instructions and exercises its functions, except that of amending the Constitution'. The Central Committee normally meets once a year. It elects a chairman and two vice-chairmen from its membership and now appoints 16 members to the Executive Committee (originally these were 12 members, since New Delhi 14 members). This body meets twice a year to implement the Central Committee's policy. Both the Central Committee and the Executive Committee have met at various places around the world in order to get better acquainted with the member churches.

Avoiding the danger of carrying out exclusively the organizational tasks entrusted to them by the Assembly, the Central and Executive Committees have concerned themselves with various basic themes which stimulated the thinking and planning of the World Council's staff. They have also issued a considerable number of statements on problems of disarmament, nuclear weapons testing, religious liberty, freedom of conscience, racial and ethnic tensions and on special political danger spots such as Korea (1950), Vietnam and Indo-China (1966, 1967, 1972), Southern Rhodesia (1966) and the Middle East (1967). The Central Committee has increasingly become the influential medium and radiation-centre of the World Council of Churches, both in regard to the ecumenical organization for which it is responsible and in its influence upon the Council's constituent bodies.

The World Council's staff is directed by a General Secretary. He is also secretary of the Central Committee and its

Executive Committee, in which capacity he is responsible for the minutes of these bodies and the implementation of their decisions. In his daily work he is assisted by a Staff Executive Group which is composed of Senior Executive staff members. By 1970 the World Council's staff consisted of well over 100 executive staff members, 160 administrative, secretarial and clerical staff and 30 persons for other ancillary services. The Council still maintains a New York office. Through frequent travel, invitations to meetings and publications, the Executive staff keeps contacts with the churches at grass-roots level and with a great number of individual Christians committed to the ecumenical movement.

Besides several mimeographed and xerographic serial publications the World Council publishes five major journals. These are: the *Ecumenical Review*, the 'official' Council's review, appearing quarterly since 1948; the *International Review of Mission*, a leading quarterly organ of missionary studies since 1912; *Study Encounter*, which provides information about studies currently being undertaken by the different Programme Units of the Council; *Risk*, a magazine for the young generation; and *Ecumenical Press Service*, a weekly publication, designed to communicate the most important ecumenical news in various continents.

The World Council of Churches is almost entirely supported by contributions from its member churches. From time to time it also receives grants from churches and foundations for specific projects. Although the wealthy churches in North America (so far still 50 per cent), Western Europe and the British Commonwealth have contributed the largest part to the operating budget, the contributions of the 'younger churches' in Asia, Africa and Latin America have increased, often representing a comparatively larger share of their members' giving. The General Budget for 1973 (annually established by the Central Committee) amounts to $1,600,000. In comparison with the large denominational budgets in the USA and elsewhere in the developed world, this amount is rather small. The Commission on World Mission and Evangelism and the

Commission on Inter-church Aid, Refugee and World Service have separate budgets, respectively $300,000 and $1,830,000 for the year 1973. The Commission on Inter-church Aid channels some 19 million dollars annually on behalf of inter-church aid agencies of member churches to help both churches and persons in distress.

I will not attempt to describe in more detail the World Council's Amsterdam (1948), Evanston (1954), New Delhi (1961) and Uppsala (1968) Assemblies. Each Assembly has published a comprehensive and detailed Official Report and various other documents. The secondary literature on the Assemblies is voluminous. Plans and preparations are being made (this usually happens three years in advance) to hold a Fifth Assembly at Djakarta, Indonesia.

Programmes and Activities

Until January 1972, when the World Council of Churches' Headquarters in Geneva was given a new structure, the Council was organized in Divisions, Departments and Secretariats. The four Divisions were: the Division for World Mission and Evangelism (created in 1961), the Division of Studies, the Division of Ecumenical Action and the Division of Inter-church Aid, Refugee and World Service, each embracing a number of departments. The Department of Finance and Administration, the Department of Information, the New York office and the Commission of the Churches on International Affairs were outside, but related to, the divisional structure.

Division of World Mission and Evangelism. This Division was the outcome of the integration of the International Missionary Council and the World Council of Churches, which was prepared over more than a decade and decided upon at the New Delhi Assembly. The International Missionary Council, established in 1921, was the result of the first World Missionary Conference at Edinburgh, in 1910, called together by the major missionary societies of the largest western non-Catholic churches. The year 1910 was later considered as the beginning of the twentieth-century ecumenical movement. The

International Missionary Council organized world missionary conferences at Jerusalem (1928), at Tambaram, Madras (1938), Whitby (1947), Willingen (1952) and in Ghana (1958). Although strong fears were expressed that the character of the World Council of Churches would be menaced by the merger with the International Missionary Council, that the world missionary movement would lose its thrust and that a joint 'mammoth organization' would be created, the final integration of the two Councils was the outcome of an inner necessity based on the conviction that both mission and unity are essential aspects of the churches.

The Commission on World Mission and Evangelism held its Second International Meeting at Mexico City in 1963 (the first in 1961). It should be noted that each World Council Division or Department is supported and guided by a Commission or a Working Committee which meets periodically to spell out the Division's or Department's policy and action. The total membership of a Commission or Working Committee and the procedures for appointing the members vary. The most significant discussions at the Mexico meeting centred upon Sections II and III, which dealt respectively with 'The Christian Witness to Men in the Secular World' and 'The Witness of the Congregation in its Neighbourhood'. The theme of the Third World Conference of the Commission on World Mission and Evangelism at Bangkok, Thailand, in January 1973 was: 'Salvation Today'. The three sections dealt with: 'Culture and Identity', 'Salvation and Social Justice' and 'Churches Renewed in Mission'.

As early as 1930 a Committee on the Christian Approach to the Jews was formed as a sponsored agency of the International Missionary Council. This Committee was reconstituted at the New Delhi Assembly as the Committee on the Church and the Jewish People, and became an integral part of the Division. It has arranged several international consultations between Christian and Jewish leaders despite considerable difficulties to bring the two faiths together. 'Most Christians are unable to engage in dialogue about faith and most Jews are unwilling to do so,' a Jewish scholar once remarked. The major aims of the Committee on the Church and the Jewish People are to warn the churches to be alert to new forms of antisemitism and to further Christian-Jewish understanding and co-operation in every way possible. The continuous political and ideological tensions in the Near East and the desperate situation of the Palestine refugees have rendered the fraternal dialogue between Christians and Jews even more complicated and more necessary than ever before. True 'trilogues' between Christians, Muslims and Jews can only be hoped for in some more distant future. A newly created Ecumenical Institute for Advanced Theological Studies, near Jerusalem, has experienced the first great difficulties in bringing Jews and Muslims together.

Two other missionary endeavours should be mentioned. At the International Missionary Assembly in Ghana, 1958, it was resolved to establish a Theological Education Fund. Its purpose is to strengthen a number of theological seminaries in Asia, Africa and Latin America and to ensure the quality of theological education in the younger churches. At the Mexico Conference (1963), the Commission on World Mission and Evangelism created the Christian Literature Fund, analogous in its organization to the Theological Education Fund, but concentrating more on an effective ecumenical co-ordination of the production of Christian literature throughout the world. I shall refer to the Christian Medical Commission, another sponsored agency of the Division of World Mission and Evangelism, in the next chapter.

The Division of Studies. This Division was composed of the Secretariat of the Commission on Faith and Order, the Department on Church and Society, the Department on Missionary Studies, the Department on Studies in Evangelism, the Secretariat on Religious Liberty and the Secretariat on Racial and Ethnic Tensions.

The Commission and the Secretariat (or Department) on Faith and Order are the continuation of the earlier twentieth-century church union movement within the context of the World Council of Churches. The origins of this movement, as of the

ecumenical missionary movement, go back to the Conference of
The International Missionary Council at Edinburgh in 1910.
Seventeen years of confidence-winning and clarification through
correspondence and consultations were to pass before the first
fully constituted World Conference on Faith and Order could
be held. There have been four World Conferences in the last
forty years: Lausanne (1927), Edinburgh (1937), Lund (1952)
and Montreal (1963). Each has been a particular stage in a
continuing conversation, and each marked another step in the
slow move to unity. As the aim of the Faith and Order movement has been to draw all churches into the ecumenical
encounter, no conference has attempted to make proposals
for church union schemes or to instruct the churches how to
proceed to reunion.

Yet, certain achievements of Faith and Order are beyond
dispute. It has been able to draw a majority of churches out
of isolation into conference, in which none was asked to be
disloyal to or to compromise its convictions. It has emphasized
the significance of ecumenical theology and biblical foundations in the whole life of the church. It has kept the churches
well informed about unity movements, negotiations about
union and church unions achieved, thus creating an ethos
conducive to other unions. For many years it has called Christians in all parts of the world to join in the annual Week of
Prayer for Christian Unity (January 18-25). It has finally reminded its constituency that co-operation is not enough; that
the fellowship of all churches in the Council is only a beginning
and not an end.

After the World Conference at Montreal (1963), several
regional Faith and Order conferences were held in Asia, North
America and Europe. The Commission on Faith and Order
(now numbering 135 members, of which 12 are Roman
Catholics) met in 1964 at Aarhus, in 1967 at Bristol and in
1972 at Louvain, continuing its task of exploring the questions
that divide the churches. The responsibility of deepening relationships with the Roman Catholic Church, admittedly a
matter for the World Council, was greatly shared by the Faith

and Order staff. The Secretariat has recently been engaged in several studies concerning the authority of the Bible, the nature of the ordained ministry, the possibility of giving a common account of the universal Christian faith and the relation between the unity of the church and the unity of mankind. To this last theme and its treatment I will refer later.

The Department on Church and Society is to some extent the continuation of the 'third prong' of the twentieth-century ecumenical movement which came to be known as 'Life and Work'. This movement was dedicated to the task of finding out how churches could assist one another in bringing their faith and religious practice to bear on the general life of society – in politics, international relations, economic conditions, education – and of exploring the responsibility of Christians for the great problems of justice and peace. The Universal Christian Council on Life and Work held two major world conferences: at Stockholm in 1925 and at Oxford, England, in 1937.

From its very beginning, the Department on Church and Society not only reaffirmed the views of the First Assembly at Amsterdam on the subject of 'The Responsible Society', but went beyond them in seeking to relate this idea to acute social problems. It launched a comprehensive study on 'Our Common Christian Responsibility Towards Areas of Rapid Social Change', and organized an International Study Conference on this topic at Thessalonica in 1959. Its great achievement was the (Third) World Conference on Church and Society, held at Geneva in 1966. Like the Stockholm (1925) and Oxford (1937) Conferences, this international gathering was carefully prepared long in advance.

Four volumes were published prior to the conference on the following themes: *Christian Social Ethics in a Changing World, Responsible Government in a Revolutionary Age, Economic Growth in a World Perspective* and *Man in Community*. The Geneva meeting stood out as the first world ecumenical conference in which laymen predominated, and as the first gathering in which participants from Africa, Asia and Latin America were equivalent in numbers to those coming from Western Europe and North America.

After the Uppsala Assembly, the Department on Church and Society launched a new study on the subject of 'The Future of Man and Society in a World of Science-Based Technology'. An exploratory conference on this topic was held at Geneva in 1970, and the Working Committee on Church and Society, at a meeting in Nemi, Italy, in 1971, continued the discussions on urgent questions concerning genetics, human environment, population, pollution, the universal urban problem, the quality of life, participation in a technological world and 'images of the future'. Recently the Department also undertook a new study on the problems and potentialities of violence and non-violence in several actual situations of social conflict.

The Department on Missionary Studies was created by the Evanston Assembly as an expression of the 'association' between the International Missionary Council and the World Council of Churches. Apart from its own programme, this Department has sought to encourage and to co-ordinate missionary research by others and has co-operated in various ecumenical studies undertaken by the Division of World Mission and Evangelism as a whole. The Department on Evangelism (also created in 1954) sponsored a few major consultations and published various studies and surveys in its field. In particular, its Study on the Missionary Structure of the Congregation was widely received and discussed by working groups in several countries and continents. In 1967 both Departments were integrated into the Department on Studies in Mission and Evangelism.

In view of frequent violations of religious liberty in several countries, the Central Committee decided in 1958 to appoint a special Commission on Religious Liberty. During its decade of existence the Secretariat on Religious Liberty published a great number of books, pamphlets, articles and working papers. It followed closely the evolution of the Roman Catholic Church's position in matters of religious liberty during the Second Vatican Council, contributed to the Council's 'Declaration on Religious Liberty' and showed deep interest in a correct interpretation and implementation of this Declaration all over the world.

The Department on Church and Society decided in 1960 to set up a Secretariat on Racial and Ethnic Tensions. Among its various projects this Secretariat sponsored an 'Ecumenical Consultation on Christian Practice and Desirable Action in Social Change and Race Relations in Southern Africa', held at Mindolo, Zambia, in 1964. The whole problem of world-wide racism was faced anew and tackled still more seriously after the Uppsala Assembly, when the Programme to Combat Racism was called into existence.

The Division of Ecumenical Action comprised the Department on the Laity, the Department on Co-operation of Men and Women in Church, Family and Society, the Youth Department and the Ecumenical Institute at Bossey (near Geneva).

The aim of the Department on the Laity was 'to be a centre of information, study and stimulation on the role of the laity, both men and women, in the life and mission of the Church'. Placing a strong emphasis on research and believing that good and creative ideas would gradually penetrate the life of the churches by their own validity, the Department organized few conferences but provided a wealth of study materials on regional and world levels which convincingly stressed that the laity, the entire community of the baptized, is the church, the true people of God. It also advocated forcefully the idea that the ministry of the laity is the major aspect of the mission of the church, whereby the church is understood as the life in society at large. How far the Department has had real impact on the World Council itself and on the various churches, marked by centuries of clerical traditions, still remains an open question. Mention should also be made of the Secretariat on Laymen Abroad, which functioned from 1962-1965 and helped to make the churches aware of the ecumenical and missionary significance of the movement of laymen from one country to another.

The title Department on Co-operation of Men and Women

in Church, Family and Society, though awkward and cumber-
some, has had the advantage of attracting attention. In contrast to the usual pattern of women's organizations, stress was
laid on the complementary nature of men and women as well
as on the enrichment of the life of the church and society
which derives from such co-operation. The Department has
dealt with many questions related to the daily lives of peoples
everywhere – those who are inside as well as outside the
church, those belonging to western societies and those who
live in other parts of the world. It sponsored several consultations and seminars such as the All Africa Seminar on the
Christian Home and Family Life, held in 1963 at the Mindolo
Ecumenical Centre, and stimulated many discussions on a
variety of subjects such as: the professional non-ordained
church worker, the admission of women to the ordained
ministry, the participation of women in churches, councils
and governing bodies, family planning, sexual ethics and co-
operation in society. Again the question may be raised whether
the communications between this Department and the Council's constituency have been very effective. The historical
records of the church show clearly that women have had even
less status and fewer rights than laymen. The burden of
centuries still weighs very heavily.

Tension and sometimes conflict between generations is also
an ecumenical reality. The Youth Department's task was to
interpret what is actually happening when younger churchmen contest the wisdom of the acknowledged leaders in the
churches and the ecumenical movement. In contrast to three
World Conferences of Christian Youth at Amsterdam (1939),
Oslo (1947) and Travancore (1952), and later regional Youth
conferences, the present younger generation in the ecumenical
scene prefers to speak about implementation rather than consultation. Although the Department's activities have not always
been looked upon with favour by older churchmen, the World
Council's constituency has learned slowly to reckon with a
rich and varied contribution from its younger members. The
Youth Department has provided many means for young people

to render service through Ecumenical Work Camps, World Youth Projects and Opportunities of Voluntary Service.

The Ecumenical Institute, located in the Château de Bossey, twelve miles from Geneva, serves two main purposes. The first is that of being a permanent conference centre where Christians of different national and denominational traditions learn from one another, gain deeper insights into the Christian faith and discover the wider horizons of the church. Some of the most creative gatherings have been the seminars which have brought together people from the same profession to consider how to make Christian faith more effective in their daily work and contacts. Such conferences have been held for journalists, educators, scientists, physicians, lawyers, biologists and leaders in business and labour-management relations. Secondly, for four months of the year the Institute conducts a Graduate School of Ecumenical Studies in association with the University of Geneva, which is open to all students, young pastors and teachers around the world who have a desire and adequate qualifications for an intensive study of ecumenical problems and want to prepare themselves for future ecumenical action in their ministry.

I will deal somewhat more extensively with the *Division of Inter-church Aid, Refugee and World Service* in the next chapter.

A New Structure

As the Uppsala Assembly in 1968 noticed that the World Council of Churches was in danger of settling more and more into a fixed pattern of operations, it instructed the Central Committee to examine and to reappraise the structure of the Council. A Structure Committee was appointed to work out a new and more flexible organizational chart. After two years of painstaking analysis and careful investigation, this Committee submitted its report to the Central Committee, which adopted it at its meeting at Addis Ababa, in 1971. As some parts of the Structure Report involve amendments to the Constitution, it will be ratified in its entirety only at the Fifth

Assembly in 1975. In the meantime the new structure was put into effect at the beginning of the year 1971.

There were various reasons for restructuring the World Council. The present crisis in the Christian faith and the furthering of new life in the church point to the need for substantial change in the method and pattern of ecumenical endeavours. As the Council is now serving many more churches in different countries and situations, the relations between the Geneva Headquarters and regional and national ecumenical organizations, which are growing in activity and size, require much closer attention. Serious financial limitations, because the contributions of the churches do not increase proportionally, demand a more effective use of staff and resources, efficiency of operation and a clearer fixing of programme priorities. At the same time, however, the Structure Committee was quite aware that the work of restructuring is never completed, nor ever will be, if the World Council is to continue 'to function as a dynamic and ever-changing body'. 'New structures,' moreover, 'will not in themselves accomplish more than those which they replace or guarantee the achievement of newly-formulated aims.'

Stating clearly that 'there is no one right structure and no theology of structure', that the problem of continuity and discontinuity can never be solved entirely satisfactorily and that therefore proposals must be pragmatic, the Committee suggested the following new structure for the Council's programmes and activities, which is now being slowly implemented. For the sake of greater clarity a diagram of this new World Council structure is added at the back of this book.

The divisional and departmental structure of the Council, which is now more than twenty years old, has now been replaced by a three-programme unit structure comprising: Faith and Witness, Justice and Service, Education and Communication. Units, sub-units and staff working groups have taken over the functions of divisions, departments and secretariats. Since the unity of the church and the content and manner of the witness of its faith in the modern world are still major concerns of the World Council, Faith and Order, World Mission and Evangelism and Church and Society have been grouped together as three sub-units of Programme Unit I. The title 'Justice and Service' has been given to Programme Unit II because of the fact that 'the great relief and rehabilitation undertakings of the churches are not a form of philanthropy or first aid which can be practised without regard to national policies, international relationships, the racial question or the economic needs of the under-developed countries'. Service of humanity cannot be separated from the struggle for justice. I will turn to the operations of this Unit in a moment.

The aim of Programme Unit III is stated as follows: 'To work with churches, councils and movements through processes of education and communication to enable persons, communities and institutions to participate as fully as possible in the changes that faith in God in Christ calls for in them, in churches, and in society.' To this end, this Programme Unit includes the various concerns and programmes previously cared for by the Division of Ecumenical Action (except the Ecumenical Institute) and the Department of Information. It is now composed of: the Staff Working Group on Renewal (including Ecumenical Youth Service and World Youth Projects), the Staff Working Group on Education (including Family Education, Laity and Adult Education, Scholarships Office and the Education Renewal Fund), the Staff Working Group on Communication (including the Press Section, Film and Visual Arts, Radio and TV, Publications, Translation) and a Sub-Unit on Relationships with National and Regional Councils. It will need more time before one can tell whether this new organizational structure can enhance better co-ordination and will prove sufficiently flexible and effective.

Relations with Other Ecumenical Bodies

From its very beginning the World Council has worked closely together with a great number of national councils of churches. Twenty-six of these councils are associated with the World Council, such as the Canadian Council of Churches, the National

Council of the Churches of Christ in the USA, the British Council of Churches, just to name the larger ones; forty-four national councils are affiliated to the Commission on World Mission and Evangelism; and thirty-four councils are in working relationships, though not in association, with the World Council of Churches. Many of these ecumenical bodies send non-voting representatives to the World Council's Assemblies and Central Committee meetings. Equally close co-operation exists between the World Council and a number of important and active regional conferences, especially the East Asia Christian Conference, the All Africa Conference of Churches, the Conference of European Churches and the Caribbean Conference of Churches.

A network of communications has also been built up between the World Council of Churches and international ecumenical bodies such as the World Alliance of Young Men's Christian Associations, the World Young Women's Christian Association, the World Student Christian Federation and the United Bible Societies. Finally, the World Council has fraternal relationships with eleven world confessional organizations, of which the Lutheran World Federation, the World Alliance of Reformed Churches and a representative of the World Methodist Council share its headquarters building in Geneva, Switzerland. The communication and co-operation between all these various bodies have not been without some success. On the other hand, an increasing number of Christians seriously questions the *raison d'être* of some of these organizations, claiming that they are either of an anachronistic nature or have been infected by the ills of bureaucracy and officialdom and only seemingly further the ecumenical dialogue. Their concerns have remained too long in the same few hands of an ageing office élite.

Relations with the Roman Catholic Church

The Roman Catholic Church has radically changed its attitude towards the ecumenical movement only during the last fifteen years. The decisive turning point came with the Second Vatican

Council and the great influence on the Council and throughout the world of Pope John XXIII. Before that time the official position of the Vatican was negative towards rapprochement with other churches. Only a number of individual Roman Catholic theologians like Yves Congar, Henri de Lubac, John Courtney Murray and Karl Rahner were interested in the ecumenical movement, and they found themselves increasingly in trouble. Abbé Couturier, who promoted the Week of Prayer for Christian Unity, remained an obscure personality in the early years. Roman Catholics tried in vain to obtain permission to attend the first two World Council Assemblies at Amsterdam and Evanston. In 1961 Rome at last agreed to the participation of official observers in the New Delhi Assembly, while in return a great number of delegated observers from various churches were invited to attend the Vatican Council. The Council's Decree on Ecumenism praised 'the ecumenical sincerity and energy of the separated brethren'. In 1965 the late Cardinal Bea announced during his visit to the Ecumenical Centre in Geneva that the Vatican had accepted the proposal to start a Joint Working Group (composed of six representatives appointed by the Vatican Secretariat for the Promotion of Christian Unity and eight from the World Council). This group was later enlarged to a membership of twenty-four and has regularly met twice a year to discuss practical collaboration, problems which cause tensions, and common concerns in the life and mission of the church.

For the first time Roman Catholics were free to address the Uppsala Assembly in 1968. The new climate of friendship and co-operation was symbolized even more clearly in the following year when Pope Paul VI visited the World Council in Geneva and called the occasion a 'prophetic moment and truly a blessed encounter', awaited for centuries. The fraternal dialogue and ecumenical collaboration continue. The mandate of the Committee on Society, Development and Peace (SODEPAX), appointed jointly by the Pontifical Commission on Justice and Peace and the World Council of Churches, has been prolonged for another three years. The Week of Prayer for Christian Unity is annually prepared by a group of World Council and Roman Catholic representatives. The Faith and Order Commission now includes twelve Roman Catholic members. Any important World Council conference or consultation is now without exception attended by a number of official Roman Catholic delegates or observers. Roman Catholic Episcopal Conferences participate fully in fourteen different national councils of churches, notably in the Netherlands, the Scandinavian countries, Sudan, Uganda, Swaziland, Melanesia, Surinam and Guyana. Perhaps the greatest progress in ecumenical action and fellowship has been made on the various local church levels in many countries.

Yet it remains extremely difficult to remove the remaining official obstacles on the road to doctrinal agreement and visible restored unity. The discussions on fuller relationships and on the eventual membership of the Roman Catholic Church in the World Council of Churches are still in their early stages. Because of its hierarchical structure and its sheer numerical weight, the Roman Catholic Church would create a whole series of new administrative and psychological problems, not to mention the theological ones, if it entered the World Council as a full member. Roman Catholic membership, in fact, would necessitate a change in the Council's constitution, alter the Council's character and create an entirely new situation with far-reaching consequences. There was a notably cautious tone in the Report of the Joint Working Group, presented to the World Council's Central Committee meeting at Utrecht in August 1972. Feelings of frustration and pessimism were also registered during the debate on the report and the procedural action. The future of the Joint Working Group is not assured, and some experts believe that for the time being the Geneva-Rome dialogue has reached a stage of deadlock.

III

Justice and Service

As I indicated in the previous chapter, the title 'Justice and Service' has been given to Programme Unit II within the new three-programme structure of the World Council of Churches, put into practice since the beginning of 1971. I purposely wish to devote a separate chapter to this Unit, because the study of its aims and functions will have some bearing on our further discussion and evaluation of the World Council, which, particularly through the services of this Unit, calls for a Christian participation in the determined international effort to reach a viable world community. The general aim of Programme Unit II has been defined as follows: 'To assist the churches in promoting justice and peace in serving men through programmes designed to advance the dignity of man and the quality of the human community.'

The Unit is divided into four sub-units, namely the Commission of the Churches' Participation in Development, the Programme to Combat Racism, the Commission of the Churches on International Affairs and the Commission of Inter-church Aid, Refugee and World Service. Among the nine functions of this Unit, four pertain to the unit as a whole; the others are related to the four sub-units. The general functions are spelled out as follows: '1. To mobilize the contribution of Christians and their churches towards a world community based on freedom, peace and justice; 2. To promote ecumenical reflections and actions on the Christian responsibility in development, racism, international affairs and other issues in contemporary world society ... 8. To develop and co-ordinate the relationships of the World Council of Churches with governments and inter-governmental agencies, and other relevant organizations and movements; 9. To help mobilize the whole people of God, irrespective of their organizational relationship to the World Council of Churches, in the fields of service, development, justice and peace.'

It should be noted that the definitions of the aims and functions of Programme Unit I (Faith and Witness) and Programme Unit III (Education and Communication) do not contain words such as 'world community', 'Christian responsibility for world society' and 'relationships with governments and inter-governmental agencies'. It is also significant that even within the aims and functions of Programme Unit II the primary emphasis is on 'the mobilization of the whole people of God', while dialogue with other religious communities and world ideologies on concerns for world community is not mentioned. The specific *Christian* contribution towards a world community is the main focus. I will discuss the implications of this fact later. Turning now to the four sub-units of Unit II I will give a brief description of each of them without going into much historical and organizational detail.

The Commission on the Churches' Participation in Development

A major theme permeated the entire World Council Assembly at Uppsala, Sweden, in 1968: 'development'. One of its six sections, 'World Economic and Social Development', urged Christians everywhere 'to participate in the struggle of millions of people for greater social justice and for world development'. The term 'development' has not yet been precisely defined. Also, the expressions 'developed' and 'developing' countries have been repeatedly questioned. For want of better terms the Council continues to use 'developed' and 'developing' to distinguish between those countries with a high gross national product and those with a low gross national product.

The Uppsala Assembly gave some content to the word 'development' when it declared in its message: 'We heard the cry of
those who long for peace; of the hungry and exploited who
demand bread and justice; of the victims of discrimination
who claim human dignity; and of the increasing millions who
seek for the meaning of life.' The major threat to world
development remains the ever-widening gap between the rich
and the poor, fostered especially by expenditure on armaments.

The year 1968 represented a climax in the World Council's
history of socio-economic concerns. But already in 1961 a
Committee for Specialized Assistance to Social Projects (SASP)
was established to provide the Council's divisions, mission
boards and churches throughout the world with technical
advice on the planning and implementation of a number of
projects designed to promote social and economic development. The members of this Committee were drawn from a
variety of professions, nationalities and denominations, and
selected on the basis of their experience in various fields of
development. SASP's advice has ranged from reorganizing
a farm school in Madagascar, leadership training in Latin
America, the re-equipping of a fruit juice bottling unit
whose profits finance a Nigerian apprentice training scheme,
the publication of periodicals in French-speaking Africa, and
colonization in the Amazon forest, to ways in which rural medical services might be increased in several Asian and African
countries. In its first section, 'Economic and Social Development in a World Perspective', the World Conference on Church
and Society in 1966 dealt extensively with the World Council's
preoccupation with troubling the conscience of sensitive
Christians over the responsibility of the 'haves' towards the
'have nots'. It called to the attention of the churches in all
continents the fact that approximately 75 per cent of the
world's resources are in the hands of about 18 per cent of the
world's population and that the trend continues for the rich
to acquire more and the poor to possess less.

The same concern for world development also found expression in *Gaudium et Spes*, the Vatican II conciliar document

dealing with the church in the modern world. It was the chief preoccupation of the papal encyclical *Populorum Progressio*. A year after the establishment of the Pontifical Commission on Justice and Peace in 1967, the World Council of Churches and the Roman Catholic Church decided to join forces and created a Committee on Society, Development and Peace (SODEPAX) with offices in the Ecumenical Centre in Geneva. SODEPAX does not organize or direct development projects, like many governmental and non-governmental agencies, but functions as a catalytic agent seeking to generate creative thinking and stimulate action in the area of international development, social justice and peace. Under its auspices an International Conference on World Development was held in Beirut, Lebanon, in 1968. The official report of the conference was published in English, French, German, Italian, Spanish and Arabic. A similar conference was held at Montreal in 1969 to update and re-examine critically the Beirut report.

Several smaller consultations and colloquia were organized in various countries, each dealing with specific issues such as acceleration of development in the second United Nations development decade, agricultural development, international monetary reform, church communication on development and a theology of development. Emphasis has been placed on education for development and peace. All SODEPAX programmes, whether on the international, regional or national level, aim ultimately at action. The Beirut report, added to other initiatives, has helped to increase the determination of Catholic and Protestant churches in several countries to work for larger Christian support for development. Various national SODEPAX committees have been formed during the last few years.

The World Council of Churches itself responded with vigour to the Uppsala emphasis and mandate in the field of development by creating a Staff Working Party on Development which in 1970 grew out into the Commission on the Churches' Participation in Development. Shortly before its creation, a Consultation on Ecumenical Assistance to Development Projects was held at Montreux, Switzerland. The title of the report

is *Fetters of Injustice*. The main objective of the Commission
is to assist churches to participate effectively in the process of
development. It understands development as a liberating process, aimed at three inter-related goals: justice, self-reliance
and economic growth, of which justice has primacy. The
poorest majority in a given country should be the agents and
immediate beneficiaries of this process. The development process is a peoples' movement aimed at enhancing their dignity,
self-reliance, social and economic well-being. It also involves
efforts in changing socio-economic and political structures
which enslave and dehumanize the poor.

In order to strive for this objective, the Commission on the
Churches' Participation in Development is in process of identifying groups related to the churches who are already promoting development concerns. These agencies and groups are
linked in a network relationship with each other and the
Commission for mutual support and dialogue. In a similar way,
efforts are being made to identify secular groups and movements which may enter into a multi-network relationship with
church-related groups around the world. The Commission
renders the following services to the World Council's member
churches and related agencies and movements: studies, education for development, documentation, technical services and
financial assistance.

As many churches and action groups have been concerned
about the issue of trade, particularly in connection with the
Third Assembly of the United Nations Conference on Trade
and Development (UNCTAD) at Santiago, the Commission
initiated an examination of this issue from the perspective of
Justice. A book entitled *Trade for Justice – Myth or Mandate*
was published in order to stimulate study and discussion at
local and national levels. A research programme 'Poverty 2000'
was launched in order to present the scale and nature of
poverty in the year 2000, drawing upon data collected on a
global level and upon certain selected micro-studies in a number of developing countries. Two developed countries, Ireland
and Sweden, are included for comparative purposes. The study

will lead to an enquiry on what must be done at different levels to accomplish minimal goals among the lowest quartile. Feasibility studies on 'The Process of People's Participation' and 'Race and Development' have also been undertaken.

In the field of development education the Commission works closely together with SODEPAX. Extensive visits to churches in twelve African countries were made to facilitate Christian co-operation in development as well as the identification of groups and agencies engaged in educational programmes. In the North Atlantic area the Commission received an overwhelming number of requests from churches and action groups for financial participation in development education programmes. Several staff members of the Commission are involved in technical activities providing extensive comments on rural development, agricultural community development, low-cost housing and fishery vocational training projects. The technical approach has developed from purely Western feasibility and evaluation processes to full participation with experts and institutions in the developing countries. To this effect a network of experts who can readily give technical advice on programmes and projects on a consultancy basis has been established and is regularly updated.

The Commission administers an Ecumenical Development Fund. Up to April 1972 this fund received, either in cash or in pledges, a total amount of $2,700,000. The money comes mainly from the churches which responded to the two per cent appeal, made by the World Council in 1970, for its income. So far the Commission has not made much effort to solicit more contributions to the fund, because it was felt that, both in terms of need and effectiveness, it would be preferable to establish first a more precise strategy which could be used as a basis for fund raising. At present a major part of the Ecumenical Development Fund is devoted to counterpart countries where the Commission is focusing its attention – at the moment Cameroon, the Caribbean, Ethiopia and Indonesia. Only these four countries were selected (two more, one in Asia and one in Latin America will be added) in order to test the strategy of the Commission in a practical way and in a limited geographical context. It is hoped to draw deeper knowledge from concrete situations so that data will be obtained as to the impact of the policies of Western countries with respect to aid, trade and investment. Indigenous agencies and movements in the Third World which are undertaking development programmes in line with the Commission's goals and principles are also supported. Finally, assistance is given to agencies and movements in a number of Western countries, which are engaged in conscientization or education for development.

It has been said that the 1960s were a 'development decade without a developing policy'. The reports have now supplied the experts with a policy. But it is a policy, many critical observers contend, for domesticating the Third World's development efforts. People talk more and more loudly of the myth of aid. Many rich countries have not even reached the 'optimum' target for development aid at one per cent of the gross national product. Under-development continues because the Third World is still the object of systematic subjugating action by the dominant nations. Developing countries are not really developing. Even if the 'third development decade' shows some better results, the basic questions, whether poor societies can obtain both development's benefits and control over the social processes which generate these benefits, and whether the developed world is truly on its way to achieving greater development, render the development debate extremely difficult. The discouraging truth is that development processes now operative impede the genesis of development for all men. There is some hope that the repressed consciousness of the Third World will emerge even more strongly with a mounting insistence on throwing off the status of dependency and subservience. Insurgent voices in Africa, Asia and Latin America increasingly articulate words like 'liberation' and 'justice' rather than aid, and show that their new concern is 'to *be* more rather than to *have* more'. The World Council of Churches shares all the perplexities of the world debate on 'development' and has as much difficulty in arriving at wise initiatives and right action as governments and their agencies.

The Programme to Combat Racism

Even before the World Council of Churches came into being, racial justice was an important issue on the agenda of several ecumenical meetings, such as the Life and Work Conference in Stockholm in 1925 and the Conference on Church, Community and State in Oxford in 1937. Since 1948, the World Council has recognized in numerous statements the increasing urgency for the Christian church to participate actively in the struggle for racial justice. At the second Assembly in Evanston in 1954, the Council stated its conviction that 'any form of segregation based on race, colour or ethnic origin is contrary to the Gospel, and is incompatible with the Christian doctrine of man and with the nature of the Church of Christ. The Assembly urges the churches within its membership to renounce all forms of segregation or discrimination within their own life and within society.' Today, this statement is still the basis for the World Council's action.

It was particularly at the Fourth Assembly in Uppsala that the world dimension of racism and its threat to world peace were recognized. 'Contemporary racism robs all human rights of their meaning, and is an imminent danger to world peace. The crucial nature of the present situation is emphasized by the official policies of certain governments, racial violence in many countries, and the racial component in the gap between rich and poor nations. Only immediate action directed to root causes can avoid widespread violence or war.'

'Racism is linked with economic and political exploitation. The churches must be actively concerned for the economic and political well-being of exploited groups so that their statements and actions may be relevant. In order that victims of racism may regain a sense of their own worth and be enabled to determine their own future, the churches must make economic and educational resources available to underprivileged groups for their development to full participation in the social and economic life of their communities. They should also withdraw investments from institutions that perpetuate racism ... The churches must also work for the change of those political processes which prevent the victims of racism from participating fully in the civic and governmental structures of their countries.'

A year later, the report of an 'International Consultation on Racism' which had been held at Notting Hill, London, itself the scene of racial conflict and violent interruption by some Black Power leaders, was presented to the Central Committee in Canterbury. The Programme to Combat Racism was established and its functions outlined as follows: (a) to mobilize the churches in the world-wide struggle against racism; (b) to express in word and deed solidarity with the racially oppressed; (c) to aid the churches in educating their members for racial justice; (d) to facilitate the transfer of resources, human and material, for projects and programmes in the field of racial justice. During the few years of its activities it was recognized that especially white racism, in its many organized ways, is by far the most dangerous form of racial conflict at present. The church itself needs to analyse and to correct its complicity in benefiting from and furthering white racism. It was further stressed that it is quite insufficient to deal with the race problem at the level of person-to-person relationships; it is institutional racism, as reflected in social, economic and political structures, which must be challenged. Therefore the combat of racism must entail a redistribution of political, socio-economic and cultural power from the powerful to the powerless. There is also no doubt that no single strategy to combat racism is universally appropriate; multiple strategies have to be worked out.

The programme priorities decided by the Commission on the Programme to Combat Racism are: (a) Action on the racial oppression of Indians in Latin-American countries; (b) African liberation in Southern Africa; (c) Land-rights for Aborigines and Maoris in Australia and New Zealand; (d) Investment analysis by the World Council and member churches;

(e) Action over global economic structures which reinforce racism and emanate principally from Western powers, particularly the USA. For a number of projects ranging from consultations on the churches' responsibility *vis à vis* the Indians in Latin America, the Cunene River Scheme on the border of Angola and Namibia, an international ecumenical team visit to North America, a conference on black and white theology, an audio-visual exhibition on 'man and racism', the Programme to Combat Racism has full responsibility. Other projects are carried out jointly with regional or national ecumenical church bodies or directly with groups of the racially oppressed.

When in 1970 the World Council's Executive Committee voted $200,000 to various organizations and 'liberation' movements from a Special Fund to Combat Racism, the Council faced a storm of protest. Some of the movements in Angola, Mozambique, Guiné-Bissao, Rhodesia and South Africa are avowedly involved in guerrilla warfare and directed towards overthrowing the white ruling government. Although it was specified that the grants are to be used for humanitarian activities with a social, health, educational or legal purpose, the World Council was accused of supporting subversive and revolutionary action. Apart from various misinterpretations of the Council's decision to promote without control the interests of thirty-two organizations and movements, several churches questioned the possibility of effectively separating the humanitarian needs of these movements from their total policy. The World Council also faced anew the problem of communication, as several of its constituent churches proved to be totally unaware of the fact that the Council had committed itself many years ago to the cause of racially oppressed peoples. The decision to create a Special Fund for the support of anti-racist projects was by no means based on a sudden inspiration, but was the outcome of a long and ever-growing conviction that words have little effect until they become deeds.

Despite consternation in several countries and great opposition which lasted for more than a year, most member churches have ratified the World Council's policy. The Central Committee voted in August 1972 to raise the target of the Fund to a minimum of one million dollars. In January 1973 the Executive Committee published a first and long list of Dutch, Swiss, UK and USA corporations directly involved in investment in or trade with South Africa, Namibia, Zimbabwe, Angola, Mozambique and Guiné-Bissao. It instructed the Council's Finance Committee and the Director of Finance to sell existing holdings and to make no investments after this date in these corporations. At the same time the Executive Committee urged all member churches, Christian agencies and individual Christians outside Southern Africa to use all their influence, including action by shareholders and the sale of investments, to press corporations to withdraw investments from and cease trading with these countries.

In connection with programme projects and the Special Fund, the Council's Programme to Combat Racism has published a series of expert profiles on FRELIMO (Frente de Libertaçao de Mozambique), PAIGC (Partido Africano de Independencia da Guinee e Cabo Verde), ANC (African National Congress of South Africa), Namibia, the Cunene Dam Scheme and the Cabora Bassa Dam, and the struggle for the liberation of Southern Africa. Other profiles are in preparation.

James Baldwin, a black American and novelist, introduced himself to the Council's Fourth Assembly as 'one of God's creatures, whom the Christian Church has most betrayed', and who had 'always been outside the Church, even when I tried to work in it'. The Christ he was presented with was a Christ with blue eyes and blonde hair, with all the virtues to which he as a black man was expected to aspire. 'I tremble when I wonder if there is left in the Christian civilizations – and only these civilizations can answer this question, I cannot – the moral energy, the spiritual daring to atone, to repent, to be born again.' This question still haunts the ecumenical movement. When the Executive Committee decided to create a Special Fund to Combat Racism the words '... and God have mercy upon us' were added to the decision. There is little doubt that the race problem and particularly the issue of white racism will preoccupy the World Council for years to come.

The Commission of the Churches on International Affairs

The Commission of the Churches on International Affairs was founded twenty-seven years ago by the International Missionary Council and the Provisional Committee of the World Council of Churches 'in process of formation', largely on the initiative of several international statesmen who were concerned that the churches of the ecumenical movement should have a direct voice in international affairs. Since its inception the Commission's main purpose has been to work to maintain and strengthen the United Nations as the only instrument – despite its weaknesses – which can provide an alternative to open warfare as a solution to international conflicts. The Commission also serves the World Council as co-ordinator of relations with the United Nations and non-governmental organizations. It maintains consultative status with the Economic and Social Council (ECOSOC) and its subordinate commissions, with the United Nations Conference on Trade and Development (UNCTAD), the United Nations Educational, Scientific and Cultural Organization (UNESCO), the United Nations Children's Fund (UNICEF), the International Labour Organization (ILO) and the Food and Agricultural Organization (FAO). The Commission also has close working relationships with the United Nations High Commissioner for Refugees (UNHCR), the Inter-governmental Committee for European Migration and the United Nations Relief and Works Agency for Palestine Refugees.* The Commission still maintains a New York office in addition to its Geneva headquarters, and some of its officers regularly attend United Nations sessions.

The Commission of the Churches on International Affairs is conscious of the fact that it is an instrument of the *churches*. It is certainly not one of the major world powers, and there-

* The Commission is a member of the Conference of Non-Governmental Organizations in consultative status with ECOSOC; it has regularly been elected to the 15-member Board, and staff members have several times served as president or vice-president.

fore cannot be an actor of equal stature on that stage. The force of the Commission is at the level of creating an awareness about the international dimensions of what are often considered isolated situations, and about the fact that the nations in which churches are located are necessarily a part of a global society with all the accompanying political implications. It has, further, as a part of the ecumenical movement, a moral force and consequently a duty to speak out whenever justice and human dignity are endangered. This does not mean that the ecumenical movement and the actions of individual churches have no political implications. It does mean, however, that the Commission can only act as a catalyst and source of stimulus for more articulate action in favour of the creation of a more human universal society. Whenever possible, it seeks to perform its task of communication and education in close collaboration with those churches and groups who are directly involved in critical political situations. The Commission clearly refrains from prescribing solutions or defining action to be taken by any particular church. Its function is to bring to issues the clarity of an international perspective which, it is hoped, will guide churches as they determine what should be their own approach.

Despite its small staff, the Commission has been able to make some significant contributions to the work of the United Nations in the fields of human rights, religious liberty, refugees, migration, disarmament and development. It was represented during the drafting of parts of the Universal Declaration of Human Rights and proposed wording especially for the Article on Religious Freedom which asserts that 'everyone has the right to freedom of thought, conscience and religion; this right includes freedom to change his religion or belief, and freedom, either alone or in community with others and in public or private, to manifest his religion or belief in preaching, practice, worship and observance'. After twenty-seven years of work the Commission is convinced that the implementation of existing international standards of human rights is still a matter of the highest priority. This conviction is derived from the study of actual situations in which these rights are either menaced or openly violated. At the same time the Commission finds it necessary to relate the provisions of existing international instruments for the protection of human rights to the struggle for social and economic justice and other fundamental rights often ignored even by governments which have formally accepted the duty of safeguarding them. An international consultation on human rights and the churches will be held before the end of 1974, and will include men and women from various parts of the world with knowledge and practical experience of the application of human rights and the results of their violation.

The Commission and its officers have also devoted almost continuous attention through the years to the problem of international disarmament, attending the successive Disarmament Conferences in Geneva and drawing attention to the planning or control of nuclear weapons and the use of atomic power for peaceful ends. A series of studies was published referring to the restraints which governments must accept and essential positive steps towards avoiding the holocaust of destruction. Parallel to endeavours to reduce the threat of war, several interventions have been made in existing conflicts and tensions as in Korea (1950), the Formosa Straits (1955, 1958), Suez and Hungary (1956), the USA-USSR involvement in Cuba, the conflict in Laos as of 1961, the continuing conflict in Algeria and the problems of Angola and Mozambique. Also included were the tensions and conflict in Cyprus (1964), the 'confrontation' between Malaysia and Indonesia and the mounting conflict in Vietnam. The Commission not only made several public statements and appeals but also, whenever possible, sent personal representatives to the leaders of warring states. Depending upon the circumstances, fundamental themes have been stressed: the avoidance of unilateral intervention; the avoidance or cessation of violence and recourse to procedures of negotiation and mediation; policies of moderation and restraint; the value of a United Nations presence in some form for keeping peace. Obviously the various inter-

ventions have had a very modest success or even none that was
immediately apparent.

In one recent conflict, in the Sudan, the World Council's
Commission, together with the All African Council of Churches, has been able to bring a final reconciliation between the
two parties of that country, riven by civil war. When the
Commission produced a background paper on the extremely
complicated situation and demonstrated to both parties through
other concrete actions that it was honestly and independently
trying to assess the problems involved, it was asked to play a
mediating role. However, this will not occur frequently; nor
does the Commission seek out such opportunities *per se*.

According to its Constitution, it is the task of the Commission 'to witness to the lordship of Christ over man and
history by serving mankind in the field of international
relations and promoting reconciliation and world community
in accordance with the Biblical testimony to the oneness of
mankind by creation'. In seeking to fulfil this task, the Commission serves the World Council of Churches, its divisions and
departments, the member churches, the national and regional
councils with which the Council is related and other international Christian bodies. The same paragraph of the Constitution also refers to the aim of serving as 'an organ in formulating the Christian mind on world issues and in bringing that
mind effectively to bear on such issues'.

One wonders why this sentence is still included in the Commission's Constitution. Is there in fact a 'Christian mind' on
world issues? Are not Christians divided among themselves
on national and international policies? It has been pointed out
that even in such a matter as the universal Christian condem-
nation of war at the First World Council's Assembly a number
of Christians were of the opinion that 'in the absence of
impartial supra-national institutions military action is the
ultimate sanction of the rule of law'. Similarly, the World
Council's approach to the race issue is not shared by several
churches in South Africa, the USA and other countries. It is
revealing that a study on a 'Christian approach to an inter-

national ethos', launched soon after the Second Assembly, was abandoned for several reasons. The expression '*the* Christian mind' is connected with the early years of the World Council of Churches as it first of all represented the churches within the Atlantic community. That time was still marked to some extent by a Christian notion of a 'free world' and the conviction that Christian culture is to be classified at the top of an international scale of objective values. If one speaks nowadays of a Christian mind on political affairs and implies that this mind can be clearly distinguished from a 'secular' mind, one cannot blame the world for distrusting the church's paternalistic and triumphalist attitude even more. If the term 'Christian mind' is still to include the notion of bearing 'the cost of Christian discipleship' in the world and expressing a radical hope against all 'worldly' hope, another expression without the definite article and the adjective 'Christian' should be coined.

Inter-church Aid, Refugee and World Service

This Commission began to be fashioned as early as 1939 when the Provisional Committee of the World Council of Churches 'in process of formation' decided to organize help for refugees in Europe. A Department on Reconstruction and Inter-church Aid, conceived of as an emergency operation to help prisoners of war, refugees and other victims of World War II, soon grew to become the World Council's largest division, rendering service to the distressed, wherever they might be, giving material aid and carrying out projects of various kind on a world scale. The Commission is an instrument of the Council's member churches and not an entity in itself, which implies that it acts as a co-ordinator between the churches, expressing their ecumenical solidarity through mutual aid in order to strengthen them in their life and mission and especially in their service to the world around them.

The Commission works closely together with several other World Council's Commissions and also affords means for consultation and liaison with governmental and non-governmental agencies through direct contacts with the Food and Agricultural Organization (FAO), the United Nations Educational, Scientific and Cultural Organization (UNESCO), the United Nations High Commissioner for Refugees (UNHCR), United Nations Relief and Works Agency (UNRWA), and through agencies such as the International Council of Voluntary Agencies (ICVA) and the Inter-governmental Committee for European Migration (ICEM). The Refugee Programme has liaisons in Geneva with the National Catholic Welfare Conference, the Lutheran World Federation and the League of Red Cross Societies, as well as with other bodies that care for refugees and displaced persons. Primary relationships outside the World Council include those which the Commission maintains with the relief, service and inter-church aid agencies of the churches, national Christian councils and regional councils of churches. It is these agencies which underwrite the Commission's service programme budget and support the projects, programmes and emergency appeals for which the Commission seeks funds, personnel or material aid.

By staff visitation, conferences and consultations, the churches and various agencies which have needs to be met are encouraged and helped in formulating these needs as projects. For many years the Commission has published an Annual List of Projects which includes a large number of projects from around the world, each conceived and examined by local churches, national councils and ecumenical groups, and recommended by the Commission to the Council's member churches. Continuous study is given to better ways of preparation and presentation of projects requested by more churches and agencies as being means of expressing ecumenical solidarity among Christians everywhere. In co-operation with the Commission on the Churches' Participation in Development, the Commission has established a Special Development Project Desk. The immediate goal is to select and handle various development projects which will serve as experiments for the churches' participation in development.

When news breaks of an acute emergency, of whatever kind or wherever it may occur, the Commission responds by immediately enquiring from the churches, councils or missionary representatives in the area about the kinds of help required. An ever-increasing number of requests for assistance in the face of natural disaster comes to the Commission. The magnitude of these disasters in terms of lives lost and property and crops destroyed is staggering, and the contributions can only be a drop in the sea of need. The Commission is frequently able to send immediate aid to the affected area even before a response of the churches to the appeal is known. The Director's emergency fund, which has been used to cable up to $20,000 within hours of an emergency being known, has been very useful. Earthquakes occurred in Iran in 1962, Yugoslavia in 1963, Turkey in 1966, Peru in 1970 and Nicaragua in 1972, just to mention the major ones. Even more frequent human suffering has been caused by numerous famines and floods. Recent man-made disasters such as in Algeria, Nigeria-Biafra, Sudan, Bangladesh and Indo-China are graved in the world's memory. In the course of all the Commission's operations, hundreds of thousands of refugees have been resettled and great material relief operations conducted, and in addition to raising vast sums of money for these purposes, it has been possible to provide the personal service of men and women qualified to deal with the highly technical, legal and social aspects of great human problems on an international scale. In certain areas of chronic emergency or long-term need, special offices have been established for the carrying out of inter-church aid and service programmes and the distribution of resources.

Unfortunately, over the last twenty years there has been hardly any diminution in the number of refugees around the world. Several thousand continue to be helped each year to resettle in countries of their choice, and handicapped refugees are given security or rehabilitation. Education figures prominently in all programmes. The focus of the Commission's concern has shifted from Europe to other parts of the world and especially to Africa. Emergency actions have been taken by the churches to give minimum requirements of shelter, clothing and food, and under the Ecumenical Programme for Emergency Action in Africa assistance was also given towards establishing rural settlements and scholarships to school and university students. The second phase in dealing with the refugee problem in Africa is the provision of individual counselling to refugees to assist in the resettlement process. In disaster areas where no Christian organization was available, efforts have been made to present the World Council of Churches to inter-governmental and governmental groups interested in refugees.

The Commission on Inter-church Aid, Refugee and World Service's most difficult task is the continuous establishment of new priorities. Before the 1960s it was relatively easy to define what corporate charitable action includes. During the last decade there has been less talk of charity than of endeavours to facilitate the sharing of resources by the ecumenical fellowship to help meet needs on behalf of humanity. The churches have not hesitated to take a greater part in governmental and inter-governmental programmes which are known as development aid and go beyond the accepted limits of charity. The current debate, however, has progressed another step. 'Aid' is not justified without genuine 'economic growth'. But true growth is conditioned by social justice. Thus the motivation behind the Commission's programmes is now stated as follows: 'aid for the sake of survival, and hopefully of some development growth, with an increasingly serious but still sidelong glance at questions of social justice'. No nation or international body can create social justice without making a direct attack on world-wide poverty. The World Council of Churches has no other choice than to continue 'to pick up the victims that fall by the way' (as it did from the very beginning), and at the same time to be in the vanguard helping to shape the direction of the journey into development. This twofold task prevents the Commission from retreating into a comfortable pietism. It also reminds the Commission that what it can do can be significant, but rarely determinative in human affairs. It is, therefore, by its faith, not an élite with some special wisdom to solve the problems of mankind.

The Christian Medical Commission

In 1967 the Central Committee decided to set up a Christian Medical Commission as a sponsored agency, accountable for its work both to the Commission on World Mission and Evangelism and to the Commission on Inter-church Aid, Refugee and World Service. This Commission works independently and deserves more attention. Medical service has always been a primary concern of the churches involved in missions in various countries. Practically every world meeting of the International Missionary Council was accompanied by an international gathering on medical policy and practice as seen from a Christian standpoint. Reviewing the legacy of Christian medical work, the World Council now realizes that many of the earlier initiatives are no longer open, and that a search for a new relevance must be made. It is now abundantly clear that the churches in mission have lacked adequate mechanisms for medical planning. The majority of their medical institutions have operated in isolation from others, and their priorities and programmes have been determined within the narrow context of their confessional and institutional walls. The time has come for all churches – Catholic, Orthodox and Protestant – to join forces and to plan their programme jointly with governmental institutions, national health centres and community services.

The medical work of the church has been historically orientated towards individual care in a hospital setting. Over ninety per cent of medical mission activities have been hospital-based. The quality of the work is undeniable. Thousands of dedicated and skilled workers have given their lives in a healing service to others. Yet today many of these institutions suffer from multiple problems: steeply rising costs, limited staff, inadequate administrative systems and obsolescence. Modern technology is making hospital care more and more expensive. Nevertheless, most Christian hospitals still seek to demonstrate a professional level of care, believing this to be an effective part of their witness. It is ironic that in doing so they very often price their services beyond the reach of the majority of the population which lives outside the urban centres and is poor. In such a situation these institutions may have not only an aura of affluence and prestige but even an image of indifference. Moreover, hospitals remain largely dependent on the donor agencies and on a highly skilled white staff, trained in Western countries. Christian missions seem to have a vested interest in their enterprises in preventing national churches from being ultimately responsible for their institutions and preventing indigenous doctors from running the hospitals themselves. It is also true that medical centres are in danger of becoming a sponge absorbing the limited surrounding medical talent, either pulling in those from other areas or preventing local people from going elsewhere.

Other shortcomings of the past approach have now been clearly recognized. The heart of medical mission practice was curative medicine. Hospitals and clinics were the vehicle of delivery. The sick and the needy were assembled once they were sick and needy. What the developing sub-tropical and tropical nations really need is preventive medicine, health education, better nutrition, sanitation, insect control and inoculations. Many health needs can and must be met in the home situation, in relationships between people, in the care of children, in living patterns and relationships to the environment. It is here that the churches are facing new tasks and need to reckon with local economic factors, local personalities and local colonial heritage. At the same time a wide and careful co-operation with governmental agencies and comprehensive health programmes is required. As long as a health service network ranging from specialized institutions and general hospitals to health centres, sub-centres, community-wide services and the home is not established, the churches risk promoting further medical underdevelopment.

The task of the Christian Medical Commission is not an easy one. The churches in the West have themselves to be educated and to be reminded more than once that Western styles of hospital-centred care and educational systems cannot be adapted to Third World national and local situations or cultural factors. It is also not easy to convince the churches of the necessity of engaging in consultations with governments, and not simply developing their own programmes for the sole purpose of keeping their institutions running at the cost of an impossible social burden on those whom they serve and train. Despite these and other difficulties, the World Council's Christian Medical Commission is convinced that Christians can face a radically new and challenging situation and find effective means whereby the ministry of healing may be directed towards the wholeness of man in his community.

IV

A Summary of Criticisms

Ever since its founding, the World Council of Churches has been frequently and widely criticized. Some of these criticisms are constructive and fair, others rather negative, sometimes due to a misunderstanding or misinterpretation of the Council's functions and actions, others again of an outspoken antagonistic and polemical nature. Most of the critical voices concern themselves with inner problems of the World Council, with the lack of effectiveness of this multifarious and complex institutional organization. Some arguments have primarily theological implications dealing with the essence of the church and the nature of the unity Christians seek among themselves. Some criticisms are based on an individualistic and anti-ecumenical attitude towards the World Council and the tendencies of the ecumenical movement to produce uniformity, contending that each single church must preserve its peculiar heritage and its own approach to the Christian faith. Although few criticisms touch upon the problems which I outlined in the first chapter and to which I shall return in the final chapters of this book, I would still like to summarize the various criticisms of the World Council of Churches in order to help the reader distinguish more clearly the different nature of my own arguments and weigh his own position in the entire debate.

The Conservative Critique

It is impossible to follow the activities and to consult the publications of the International Council of Christian Churches and the American Council of Churches 'without concluding that they constitute nothing more honourable than a smear campaign'. Both organizations are the creation of one American, Dr Carl McIntyre, also the founder of his own Bible Presbyterian Church. Knowing that it is not very difficult to rouse violent anti-ecumenical feelings in the very conservative Protestant camp, he organized the American Council of Churches to combat the Federal Council of Churches (the predecessor of the National Council of the Churches of Christ in the USA). Later the International Council of Christian Churches was set up with the very same purpose of attacking the World Council of Churches. It is not an over-simplification to say that both organizations represent isolated groups and that their assertions are totally unfounded.

Believing in the absolute infallibility and inerrancy of the Scriptures and claiming to preserve the theological essentials of historic orthodoxy against modernism, this fundamentalist movement has only one aim : to save Christians from the grave errors and perils of the 'ecclesiastical United Nations'. In a rather strange combination, the leaders of the World Council are constantly accused of being 'modernists', 'Romanizers' and 'Communists' at one and the same time. Particularly after the Second Vatican Council, when the Roman Catholic Church opened its doors, the World Council of Churches was even more suspected of 'selling out the Protestant Reformation' and of returning to the bosom of the Mother Church. When the Russian, Rumanian, Bulgarian and Polish Orthodox churches became full members of the World Council in 1961, it was the Kremlin which, after years of abuse of the Council as a 'façade for Western imperialism', allowed these state-controlled churches to join the World Council. Since that date there has been no more doubt in McIntyre's mind that the Ecumenical Centre in Geneva is a communist-inspired organization and a subversive Moscow agency.

The Inter-denominational Foreign Mission Association also has a strongly evangelical doctrinal platform and is generally

regarded as being in the fundamentalist tradition, but its outlook is less politicized. The Evangelical Foreign Missions Association, another American missionary organization, the
Southern Conference of Baptist Churches in the USA and the
Evangelical Alliance in Britain, with the corresponding
national alliances affiliated to the World Evangelical Fellowship, also share some of the hesitations and suspicions of the
fundamentalist bodies previously mentioned, but practise a
policy of non-co-operation and of staying aloof from the World
Council. Like the Southern Baptists, the Missouri Lutherans,
in contrast to other Lutheran churches, feel that ecumenical
co-operation must be excluded before a conclusive doctrinal
verbal agreement has been reached. Holding to their belief in
spiritual experience, various Pentecostalist churches consider
the spirituality and operations of the World Council to be
boring and meaningless. Fundamentalists and conservative
evangelicals still have a considerable influence, particularly on
the 'younger churches' in the Third World. Besides these
churches, mention should be made of several hundreds of
fringe sects which show no interest whatsoever in the progress
of the ecumenical movement. Most of these conservative
Christians have at least a few ideas and concerns in common:
individual conversion, adult baptism, the literal inspiration and
infallibility of the Bible, an all-out opposition to liberalism
and clericalism, a rejection of a 'super-church', and very often
a seemingly neutral attitude towards political and social
matters. Unfortunately all ultra-conservative churches and sects
fail to realize that the universal message of their Lord Jesus
Christ can neither be reserved for the conversion of individual
souls nor limited to the spotless life of a number of small Christian communities. If the Bible is correctly understood only by
less than one per cent of all Christians, then surely something
must be wrong with their 'correct' interpretation of the
Scriptures.

The Passionate Argument for Reunion
On the opposite wing to anti-ecumenical believers there are

Christians who not only are committed to the ecumenical movement but who continue to plead with great passion for an acceleration of the process of reunion of the churches. They are, so to speak, right on the other side of the 'ecumenical fence'. They have some charismatic qualities, like those of the first pioneers in the ecumenical movement and the first leaders of the World Council of Churches in its early days. Their argument runs as follows. During its fifty years of existence the Faith and Order movement has worked hard to bring many churches together, and not without success. It is true that its Commission and its Secretariat did not succeed in defining the ecclesiological (meaning: relating to the theological doctrine of the church) nature of the World Council of Churches and that even today no single concept of the unity of the church is accepted by all churches. But the best representatives of all Christian churches have met on numerous occasions, issuing a series of consensus statements on the reality and significance of the ecumenical fellowship, despite their ecclesiological disagreements. After centuries of separation and mistrust the churches have finally come together and solemnly pledged that they will stay together.

Why is it then that the World Council's great concerns for a united church are increasingly marked by frustration, resignation and confusion? Why is there louder talk than before of the meagre results of all the well-prepared Faith and Order conferences? Why have so relatively few church unions taken place? How is it possible that after several decades of living together the distressing problem of intercommunion has in no way been solved? The World Council cannot be compared, after all, with the United Nations. The sovereign states which are members of this organization have only just started to respect each other and to learn slowly how to build up the peaceful world community of peoples which is so urgently needed. It is also true that in the political realm internationalism is threatened by a resurgence of nationalism. Nations seek to affirm their national identity and are still more concerned with their own prosperity and security than with sacrificing a part of their welfare for the family of men. The Council, on the contrary, represents a family of churches which confess Jesus Christ as Lord and Saviour, and is dedicated to the task of serving him and not a worldly authority or fallible power. Consequently the common origin and the lasting kinship of the churches are beyond dispute. Why then has the ecumenical movement not yet resulted in a compelling and dramatic manifestation of the oneness of all people who believe in the Lordship of Jesus Christ?

The reunion enthusiasts probe into the heart of this problem. Their search for the cause of failure is intensive and desperate. Perhaps something went wrong, they ask themselves, from the very outset of the movement. The First Assembly at Amsterdam already emphasized that the 'first and deepest need is not new organization, but the renewal, or rather the rebirth, of the actual churches'. Since 1948 World Council documents have referred over and over again to the inseparable relation between unity and renewal. Unity will not come except through shared renewal. Vice versa, unity is the only ecumenical way to renewal. Apparently a deep and widespread renewal in the life of the churches has not taken place. Ecumenists now wonder whether transformation failed to reach the inner being of the Christian churches because they lacked spiritual depth or because their ecclesiastical structures were rigidly institutional, or even for both reasons. Orthodox, Anglicans and Protestants all speak about 'radical renewal' in their own way, but in the last resort no confessional community envisages a change in its basic church pattern. Ultimately, then, the World Council of Churches does not seem to differ so much from an organization like the United Nations. As, in world politics, internationalism has led to a new defence of nationalism and a vigorous defence of the interests of autonomous states, so the internationalization of Christianity has been curbed by a strengthening of confessional identities and a consolidation of various church traditions. The World Council of Churches seems to serve as an international façade to cover up the isolationism of ecclesiastical bodies, just as the

United Nations functions as a palliation for the selfish affairs of nations.

The loyal supporters of the ecumenical movement still face another probing question. Could it be true that from now on it does not make much difference whether the process of reunion is accelerated or not? Many Christians, particularly but not exclusively among the young generation, maintain that doctrine and church order no longer play a divisive role in church reunions. Faith and Order has fought a long and courageous battle to bring the confessions together, but that battle has now become a sham fight. A new battle has started on a quite different front. Not confessional issues, but political and social problems divide the churches. The zeal and hope of the reunion advocates, so strong and confident in the beginning and at the height of the ecumenical movement (perhaps until 1961), are now overshadowed by tragic feelings of impotence and failure. The delay of more official and visible unity has now resulted in its loss.

The 'Death of Confessionalism' Issue

Even twenty years ago confessionalism was an inherited structure of the ecumenical movement and a clear issue for the World Council of Churches. Now, however, Anglicanism, Methodism, Lutheranism, Calvinism and other confessions have lost much of their steam and are vanishing phenomena. This opinion is widely shared by so-called 'simple' and 'unsophisticated' Christians in many countries. Hardly anybody, they reason, still wants to swim against the tide which has swept the historical confessions together. Purity of doctrine, mixed marriages, confessional schools, eucharist versus Lord's supper are now old points of controversy. Confessionalism scarcely plays any role in the daily life of Christians. There is, on the contrary, a clear desire to step across the historically conditioned confessional boundaries.

In the realm of the church's worship, too, more attempts should be made, these impatient Christians agree, to overcome the confusion of confessionally tainted liturgies and services.

Even the Annual Week of Prayer for Christian Unity, still celebrated with much expectation and fervour some years ago, is
now attended with less enthusiasm and more boredom. Instead
of praying together only one week per year Christians everywhere wish to participate throughout the year in church services which are not conditioned by an exclusively confessional
tradition and do not take place in an irrelevant denominational
setting. A free choice of religious education for children born
of mixed marriages, common catechisms, joint mission and full
participation in each others' celebration of the eucharist are
now conceivable as the confessional differences have died out.
In their daily faith many ordinary Christians have actually
carried the reunion of the church into effect. This does not
mean that each Christian shares his fellow-Christian's points of
view. On the contrary, one is aware of the fact that divergences
of opinion, which are small in comparison to the classical confessional differences, can and should enrich the same Christian
community. Thanks to the withering away of a confessional
consciousness, Christians of quite different backgrounds can
now live together in a daily life of praise, witness, learning and
service.

The issue of the extinction of confessionalism is also
approached from another angle and a different conclusion is
reached. A considerable number of Christians, more fully
orientated towards the problems of modern society, claim that
nowadays political positions rather than confessional attitudes
continue to divide the churches. Each denomination is split
into a camp of politically (more) conservative and a camp of
politically (more) radical Christians. Neo-Orthodox, liberal,
existentialist and 'death of God' theologians can live peace-
fully together, but representatives of an unpolitical brand of
Christianity and advocates of revolutionary change in society
clash head-on. Only recently have we clearly come to realize,
progressive and radical Christians argue, that no institution,
including the church, can be politically neutral or uncon-
cerned. Every personal and collective existence is political.
Every church, too, is mixed up with a political order, whether

it is conscious of this fact or not. The gospel, therefore, cannot be politically neutral. The political innocence and harmlessness of any Christian community is a myth. The New Testament message of justice and reconciliation is authentic only if its messengers take up a political stand and declare themselves in solidarity with the oppressed and exploited classes of society.

Consequently, it is pointed out, the partners of the ecumenical dialogue have changed. An Anglican now has little interest in meeting a Baptist or a Lutheran as such, nor does a Protestant attach much value to a conversation with any Roman Catholic, or vice versa. As the political dividing line cuts right through all confessions and denominations, many Christians, suspicious of political involvement and aggressive social action, easily get together. Similarly, those who join with conviction in the battle for social and economic justice seek and find a wide fellowship. They soon realize that their passion for liberation and social justice can bring more people together than the concern for a world-wide eucharistic fellowship. They may accuse their conservative brethren of failing to see that even the eucharist can be a sign of division rather than of union, because a deeper solidarity is experienced with those inside other churches and sometimes outside the church of Jesus Christ than with fellow Christians who partake in the same bread and wine of the Lord's table. On the other hand, the 'rightist' camp might blame the 'leftist' camp for having turned from being a fellowship of Christians, concerned to serve the interests of the church, into a group bringing pressure on Christians for certain social and political activities. Whatever the validity of this third argument may be, there is surely a great need for a new kind of ecumenical dialogue between 'non-politically' minded and 'politically' minded Christians. It remains to be seen whether the World Council of Churches can and will play a specific role in promoting this difficult dialogue.

The 'Establishment' Issue

The word 'ecumenical movement' is widely preferred to the word 'ecumenism'. The latter suggests an intellectual system or an ordered body of ecumenical teaching, and contains no demand for a way of life. It is by a movement that Christians are swept up and carried along. The World Council of Churches was created to drive forward the twentieth-century ecumenical movement. To what extent have the established churches been influenced by the World Council? Has the Council itself become an establishment within an established ecumenical movement? Benevolent and malicious critics both have enough opportunity to express their fears that the large organization at Geneva has tended to get bogged down in a centralized bureaucracy. There is indeed little doubt that the Council's Headquarters have become a sizeable and well-established institution. Not only does it now employ five times as many executive, administrative and secretarial staff as in its early years after 1948, but it has developed an institutional style of life and work of its own. From year to year a detailed programme of staff meetings and working groups is worked out by a number of senior officers of whom several have worked in the service of the Council for ten years or more. Each calendar year is filled with Unit and Sub-Unit meetings, Commission meetings and sessions of the Executive and Central Committee. Moreover, international conferences of one or another kind are carefully prepared and take place every year. The Council thus moves from meeting to meeting, from study group to study group, from conference preparation to conference preparation, from conference to conference, from post-conference evaluation to post-conference evaluation, from sharing of concerns to sharing of concerns. The traffic of sessions never ceases and the same staff keeps the traffic going.

All the World Council's business meetings are conducted in a Western parliamentary style. With its stress on representative democracy, the Anglo-Saxon parliamentary system is a procedure suited to bringing about an agreement on delicate matters where no unanimous decision can be reached. The Council, inasmuch as it is a council of separated churches, is necessarily dependent upon institutional structures which can produce consensus-statements. The Western influence is not only dominant in Assembly procedures but permeates the Central and Executive Committee and the Council's occidental organization itself. Much work is done through policy reference committees, nominations committees, credentials committees, finance committees and several other committees, with all the procedural operations that that involves – recommendations or decisions arrived at, referred back to plenary sessions, amended, re-debated in the respective committees and so on. Each Assembly, Central or Executive Committee publishes a full official report of its meeting and actions. Frequently other printed publications are prepared and distributed in the three official languages. Most of these records and reports are consulted within a small circle of Geneva-orientated specialists. The Council's constituent bodies and Christians in the congregations themselves have little or no notion at all and do not care how the Council's machinery runs from month to month and from year to year. Many conference minutes and consultation reports are indefinitely shelved in the Headquarters' Library and never reach national or local church life.

More than once suggestions have been made for decentralizing and regionalizing the central establishment in Geneva. There has been a proposal to create regional offices of the World Council in the various continents and to reduce the top-heavy Geneva Headquarters to a co-ordinating office and communication centre of regional organizations. The simple question: 'What should be reckoned as a region?', however, is itself a stumbling block. The old answer: Asia, Africa, Latin America, North America, Australia and Oceania, and Europe is unsatisfactory. One Asian office, for example, could not possibly meet the need to strengthen Asian participation in the ecumenical movement. The various churches in this vast continent face quite different situations and have different national problems and concerns. To consider Scandinavia or French-speaking West Africa as regions would still create insurmountable obstacles. The major problem is, however, how to avoid the danger that even regional offices will turn into micro-establishments which do not themselves reflect the consciousness, the interests and the commitments of the regional constituency. It has been pointed out that even the All Africa Conference of Churches and the East Asia Christian Conference, to name two well-established regional councils of churches, are as unknown as the World Council to the majority of Christians in these continents. Their ecumenical conferences, consultations, studies and documents, too, have little or no impact on the lives of many of the committed church members. Their offices, too, are run by an élite, so absorbed in the tasks of administering the unwieldy structures and institutions inherited from the West, that it has neither time nor the energy to engage in the complex task of educating and communicating with the Christian masses. Further down the scale, too, national councils of churches, and particularly the larger and older ones, suffer more or less from the ills of paternalism, bureaucracy and isolationism, perpetuated by their fixed institutional structures.

It has been frequently pointed out, however, that the World Council of Churches is aware of its institutional predicament and willing to re-examine its structures and actions. The Council indeed welcomes healthy and corrective criticism from the outside, as it knows that it has reached, like any other movement, the critical phase between the uncontrolled dynamic of its birth and the time of becoming institutionalized. There is little doubt also that the Genevan housekeeping compares quite favourably to the administration of various international organizations all struggling with problems of bureaucratic procedures, decentralized organizational patterns, effective communication on the national and local level, staff selection and personnel management from a supranational perspective. Yet even the most constructive critics are no longer sure whether 'the historic paradox of the World

Council as both a council of churches and a dynamic frontier movement' has been maintained, even to a small degree, to the present time. The dividing line between spontaneous movement and permanent organization seems to have been definitely crossed and there is no return. Thus the *élan* of the first decades has been smothered in a firmly shaped body, and insufficient men are available to bridge the gulf between movement and institution. The new Council's structure, designed to increase the flexibility of the organization and the 'manoeuverability of the staff', cannot change these facts. No wonder, it is concluded, that many impatient and disillusioned Christians, who are not familiar with the considerable changes in the relations between the churches between 1948 and 1961, due to the catalytic function of the Council, now substitute a 'Third Ecumenical Movement' for the 'established movement at a deadlock'. I will refer to their argument later.

The 'Third World' Issue

At the inaugural Assembly in Amsterdam in 1948, only a few churches from Asia, Africa and Latin America were represented. Although many more 'younger churches' and newly established independent churches joined the World Council in the following two decades, the international church movement is still not fully ecumenical, in so far as in its leadership and in the composition of its meetings, the older churches in Europe and North America continue to hold a dominant position. The Orthodox Churches, virtually confined to the Northern hemisphere and thinly spread outside Eastern Europe, the USA and Near East, have to some extent re-accentuated the white predominance. The long and difficult dialogue with the Roman Catholic Church hierarchy also partly diverts attention from a truly effective Third World participation in the World Council of Churches.

The Council, however, as critical voices admit immediately, is very much conscious of the 'North-South' tensions, and sincerely wants the voices of Asians, Africans and Latin Americans to be heard as never before. The World Conference on

Church and Society at Geneva in 1966 was a great success partly because of wide and active Third World participation. The third Chairman of the Central Committee, Dr M. M. Thomas, is an Asian from the Church of South India and the Council's third General Secretary, Dr Philip Potter, is a Methodist, born and educated in the West Indies. Recent World Council meetings have shown very plainly that non-European and non-American interventions and criticisms are becoming more and more articulate and are essential to any further progress in the ecumenical movement. Some highly qualified persons from the Southern continents now fill important positions on the Geneva Headquarters staff.

It nevertheless remains difficult, according to the defenders of the Third World interests, to bring out the potential non-Western impact on the World Council and to correct the imbalance in its total executive staff. Non-Westerners still have the disadvantage of not speaking one of the three official languages as their mother tongue, nor can they acquire more than one of the official languages as easily as many Westerners. Frequently they also do not meet the educational and technical standards which are required for the smooth running of a Western-type international organization. There is even a great danger that those who have come from the Southern hemisphere to the Council sooner or later adapt themselves to the Western organizational machinery and learn the rules of parliamentary procedures and group debates to such a degree that they no longer figure as outspoken Third World representatives.

It is just as difficult, the critics contend, to introduce more specific non-Western concerns and problems into the World Council's programmes. The Third World, generally speaking, can make a particular contribution to the creation of a different sense of proportion in doctrinal and theological matters. Its voices are also most important, since they represent Christians who find themselves in most countries in a clear minority position *vis-à-vis* other religions, traditions and cultures. Third World Christians can further demonstrate convincingly that

what are at stake are not traditional inter-confessional issues
but problems of a new interpretation of the Christian faith in a
multi-religious and multi-cultural milieu. Finally, they can help
the Council to face the problems of world poverty and under-
development from their side, and not from the point of view of
a Western spectator and benefactor. But only time will tell
how and when many Christians from the 'developing' parts
of the world will state their case forcefully and perhaps change
the course of the ecumenical movement.

The Clergy versus Laity Argument

The World Council of Churches, like its constituent bodies,
has been a clergy-ruled and clergy-dominated institution. Regardless of many good intentions and a whole series of discussions and studies on the rediscovery of the role of the laity
during the last twenty years, it is still mainly ordained minis-
ters, bishops and church officials who are delegated to the
Council's General Assembly and serve the Central Committee
and the various World Council commissions as top policy-
makers and expert advisers. There are few Christians in and
outside the Council who do not share this criticism.

Looking, however, at the official reports of the four Assemblies themselves (not to mention hundreds of other publications), one is surprised how vigorously and tenaciously the
participation of the laity in all church life has been defended
and spelled out. Already at Amsterdam it was stated that 'the
laity constitutes more than 99 per cent of the church' and that
'the churches are too much dominated by ecclesiastic officialdom, clerical or lay, instead of giving vigorous expression to
the full rights of the living congregation'. The Evanston
Assembly underlined the fact that it is not enough 'to secure
for the laity some larger place or recognition in the Church';
its ministry springs from the rediscovery of the true nature
of the church as God's people. 'The laity stand at the very
outposts of the kingdom of God.' The New Delhi Assembly
rejoiced in the work and achievements of the Council's Department on the Laity and encouraged further investigations on the

witness, the worship and service of the *whole* church of Jesus Christ. Laymen and laywomen are everywhere in a much better position than clergymen 'to provide a two-way channel of communications between church and world'. At Uppsala in 1968 it was specifically recommended that future World Council assemblies should be improved and ways be considered to ensure a far greater participation of laymen, women and youth.

The fact that full and equal involvement of Christian women on the local church level and in the world-wide ecumenical movement has been stressed over and over again is another theory that cannot be overlooked. There are numerous references in Assembly reports and in many records of the Department on Co-operation of Men and Women in Church and Society to the urgent need to encourage women to make their various and specific contributions to the total life of the churches. Women should share fully in the opportunities and responsibilities of church membership and become an ever-present and dynamic force in the World Council's activities.

Despite the World Council's long, sincere and intelligent plea for a change of traditional ecclesiastical behaviour, it can be seen that ordinary church members in all denominations are still satisfied to carry a minimum responsibility. Many Christian men and women do not want 'to play a key role in every area of life' but prefer to render a simple lay-service under the guidance and supervision of the ordained and 'professionally' experienced pastor or priest. Again, notwithstanding several official World Council recommendations and resolutions to increase the number of laymen and women in its own international gatherings, it still frequently happens that during the actual conference it is shamefully admitted, with many regrets and excuses, that 75 per cent of the participants are ordained, 95 per cent of male sex and 60 per cent over the age of 50. Apparently it takes more than twenty-five years and perhaps at least another twenty-five years to change dogged attachments to traditional religious customs, church models and sociological groupings, to which the church

attached the label of divine order centuries ago and which
ordinary church members do not wish to see disturbed.

The 'Grass-Roots' Issue

The following criticism is closely related to the previous point.
The first General Secretary of the World Council remarked
not long ago that the ecumenical enterprise is 'still too much
an army with many generals and officers, but with too few
soldiers'. He continued: 'The ecumenical movement is not
sufficiently rooted in the life of the local congregations.' There
are facets to the 'grass-roots' problem. On the one hand
ecumenical pioneers have reminded the church from the beginning that the awareness of a world-wide fellowship and a
world-wide service is created and nourished at the very 'down
to earth' level of the local congregation. On the other hand
the real test of the adequacy of the World Council of Churches
is whether it is able to inspire the local and parochial experience with all that the word 'ecumenical' signifies. One can also
say that the grass-roots question is largely a problem of bilateral
communication: from the bottom to the top and vice versa.

The local church situation is undoubtedly quite different
from the years before World War II. Many local church councils have been founded in many countries, particularly in the
Atlantic area, promoting joint worship services, joint study
groups, joint action in Christian aid and missionary service,
joint local social and political action. Ecumenical relationships
have been widely extended beyond an occasional friendly
getting together. It has also been pointed out that in a considerable number of parishes clerical domination has been
replaced by clerical-lay partnership and sometimes by almost
exclusive lay initiative, in spite of the fact that the clergy
resented the laity taking a lead in ecumenical affairs. But local
ecumenical co-operation, sharing and action requires commitment in terms of energy, time and money. 'Effective ecumenical
action is not something which can be added to normal denominational work. People, clerical and lay, are busy, and
ecumenical activities will have to take the place of regular

commitments.' Moreover, the creation and training of inter-
denominational team ministries, the construction of ecumenical church centres and the realization of reciprocal intercommunion remain thorny questions. It should not be
supposed that all radical ecumenical experiments offer satis-
factory or lasting solutions. While certain problems are
solved, new ones arise on the horizon at the same time. Grass-
roots ecumenism can still be criticized by raising the delicate
question whether the parish is really caught up in the renewed
life of the church universal and ready for a costly participation in the ecumenical movement. The obligation of communicating with 'the top' is not often inscribed on the local
agenda.

How far has the World Council of Churches been able to
inject its concerns and ideas into local church life? The
numerous discussions on this subject have been animated,
sometimes frustrating but persistent. The term 'crisis of communication' has become a standard expression. It is still not
generally recognized that communication is not a matter of
techniques or of an enormous centralized and well-organized
department of information. The present channels of communication, the critics argue, are still first of all the 'hierarchical' ones; the direction of information is mainly from the
Geneva Headquarters to the denominational offices and church
officials. Information concerning the church throughout the
world and the most significant contemporary aspects of the
ecumenical movement is not sufficiently edited for it to be
used effectively at local level. There is little wisdom in
encouraging denominational journals and parish magazines to
make imaginative use of books, pamphlets, news sheets and
audio-visual aids poured out by the World Council and various
national councils of churches. The materials needed by the
local churches, involved in a process of study and ecumenical
parish education, are first of all fact-sheets, brief summaries
of work being done elsewhere and short reports of local and
national meetings connected with the common search for
priorities.

To this effect a much more fluid two-way traffic should be created : regular visits by the Geneva staff, current information sheets dealing with the facts necessary for local ecumenical leadership, central files connected with regional desks in Geneva grouping the correspondence with single churches together, and a greater concentration both in the churches and at the Geneva end on a following-up of important Assembly decisions.

The 'Third Ecumenical Movement' Argument

This argument has been formulated by spontaneous and informal groups, 'diaspora movements', so-called underground churches and individuals, all agreeing that the World Council of Churches and the official ecumenical movement have failed in their endeavours and have no real future. Naturally, the Council and its constituency cannot accept this criticism, but it frequently ignores the existence of some extreme pressure groups and movements.

The first ecumenical movement, so goes the reasoning, was realized as a co-operation between gifted individuals in the churches. Great pioneers like Nathan Söderblom, J. H. Oldham, John R. Mott, Marc Boegner, William Temple, George Bell and Willem A. Visser't Hooft were outstanding men of vision who joined the ecumenical movement because they were personally convinced of its necessity and its success. The collaboration of these men and others, engaged in Faith and Order, Life and Work, the International Missionary Council, the World Student Christian Federation, facilitated the creation of a centripetal movement towards an established co-operation in a council of churches to which each church would bind itself and back the results of the co-operation.

The second ecumenical movement began in 1948 with the inauguration of the World Council of Churches. The task was now to see to it that the ecumenical movement became a movement of the churches and that adequate structures were developed. The creation of the World Council meant an awakening among the leadership of the churches to the necessity of

the ecumenical movement, but at the same time a 'churchifica-
tion' of the movement itself. Faith and Order became the
instrument through which the actual empirical churches and
confessions were brought together. Mission now implied the
missionary obligation of the churches, no longer that of the
missionary societies. Thus church officials took over 'to ensure
that many of the decisions of the World Council are implemented in the life of the bodies in which they carry
responsibility'.

The third ecumenical movement arose largely outside the
World Council of Churches in the sixties. It claims to be
characterized by a true experience of unity and to be engaged
in a true dialogue with the world, not in conversation *ad intra*
between churches and ecclesiastical traditions. It has also re-
discovered some of the depths of human life, of mystery, of
the feast and the cult. All this has been lost in the institutionalized fellowship of the World Council, as there is little
participation in its life from the rank and file of the churches.
Unfortunately the Council is even unwilling to learn something
from the experiences of unity existing *de facto* among Christians in the third ecumenical movement. It was an instrument
of the vanguard and a true expression of the ecumenical movement. Now it comes trailing behind. The structured fellowship
of the churches in the World Council leads nowhere. A new
wind is chasing away the clouds of boring conformity and
ecclesiastical ecumenical indifference which have hung over the
last decade. Many new spontaneous and radical ecumenical
groups want to replace endless discussions and statements by
explicit commitment and convincing action. Their heroes are
Camillo Torrès, Helder Camara, Martin Luther King, 'Che'
Guevara, Regis Debray, Alexander Solzhenitsyn and many
others who suited the action to the word. Ecumenism is always
a risk, they say, and has nothing to do with wise and prudent
compromise.

Most of these so-called 'post-ecumenical' Christians, and
especially the committed young people, are no longer prepared 'to give their time to serve ecclesiastical institutions'.

They want 'to serve communities of men with real needs'. Any integration into the structures of the official ecumenical movement is strongly resisted. Others, however, stay on the fringe of the World Council and consider themselves as a constant challenge to the ecumenical establishment. They continue to be pressure groups speaking to the churches and pushing them forward to realize a faster growth and more real unity, and to arrive at new priorities for action and thought. One can debate at great length whether the 'third ecumenical movement' is indeed an advancing and spreading movement. There are signs that certain communities and groups have themselves become entangled in a process of institutionalization in order to give public expression to their existence and conduct. Some constituted order of organization seems to be indispensable for their survival. It is further a question whether the experience of an all-embracing unity is as real as is suggested. Many communities are totally ignorant of each other and do not even desire to communicate with one another. Ecumenicity often ends at the border of local or national concerns. It is further doubtful whether the third ecumenical movement will ever have such an internationally contagious effect and such a global impact on a great number of Christians as the second one. Finally, many of the older and newly-formed groups remain diffuse and inefficient because they gravely lack a sense of history. Neither the unity of the church nor the unity of mankind can be aspired to by by-passing the historically conditioned and historically rooted institutions of our time. Whatever the deep experience of unity in all third ecumenical movements may be, it remains in many cases an isolated and self-contained experience.

The Need for Deeper Sociological Analysis

This final argument is not so new as some of the previous ones. At intervals, theologians and sociologists have pointed out that the ecumenical movement should also be viewed in an indirect way by analysing and studying not just the life of the churches but the course of a specific social process.

After all, the ecumenical movement has arisen and developed in a given society and in a given period and is therefore a product of social history. Thus it is necessary 'to examine the tendencies towards rapprochement to confessions and of the divided Christian communities in the framework of the relationships between church and society'. Following a sociological method of analysis, one can make several observations and arrive at some conclusions.

Facing the population explosion in the non-Christian world and the fact that the secularization of the 'Christian West' continues, twentieth-century Christianity has found itself in a minority position. In the process of estrangement between the church and the world, the world increasingly affirmed its autonomy of culture over against the church which for centuries succeeded in keeping the world under its tutelage. Consequently the ecumenical movement was initiated as a response of the churches to mounting external pressures and threats. It is only in this century that a world civilization has been born and that this 'civilization is in the process of becoming a planetary phenomenon'. The nostalgia of a Christian universality, still expressed in the early twentieth-century missionary movement, is now superseded by the secular dream of creating a united humanity. Facing the rise of a world society which aims at its own universalization through science and technology and is developing a new common language and, for the first time, a set of common beliefs among all men, the churches had no other choice than to close their ranks.

Modern global civilization, to be sure, faces its own contradiction and produces its own universal conflicts. The disasters of the two World Wars, the battle of Western democracies against Nazism and Fascism, the anti-imperialist struggle of the Third World, the antagonism between the communist blocs, all clearly indicate that the world society has passed through a series of deep crises and will not be spared other disruptions and clashes on a world scale. But precisely for that reason the churches became aware that they must unite, and in this case not only as a means of common defence against the secular world, but by calling attention again to the heritage of their Christian visions and values. Despite the modern world's aspirations, the unity of mankind cannot be as easily realized as the unity of the church. Secular world civilization has helped and intensified the successful development of the ecumenical movement.

It is understandable that many churches and individual Christians have reacted negatively to this kind of sociological analysis of religious phenomena, questioning the competence and objectivity of the social sciences. But 'to say that the ecumenical movement was born in a given sociological context, to say that its birth and its development have been favoured, influenced and orientated by a certain number of sociological facts, does not mean at all to pronounce a judgment on the significance of the movement'. This is indeed the real problem. The genesis and growth of the World Council of Churches, it is quite true, is an event conditioned by the interplay of certain religious factors. The *raison d'être* of the Council can only properly be grasped in the realm of theological understanding. But a valid theological interpretation of the ecumenical movement cannot ignore the historical context of the motivation for ecumenical mobilization.

There is much evidence that the churches have not really 'profited' from the sociological conclusion that the unity of Christians and the tendency towards an international synthesis of Christian values are of great importance to modern Western society. Precisely here the church could have learned that Christian unity does not have real meaning in itself, that its historical reality is judged, that it must be freed from the past, 'die to itself' and become a true witness of the kingdom of God. Precisely because there is much truth in the observations of religious sociologists, the World Council's way to serious self-examination and self-criticism has been paved. But for some reasons ecumenical Christians continue more or less to ignore the sociological context of their movement and consider that modern sociological interpretations do not get to the roots of the World Council's being and outlook. The result is that instead of speaking with a prophetic voice to the present secular and religious situation, the churches are still too much occupied with joining small Christian ghettoes together to form one large Christian ghetto. Hence they demonstrate, as religious sociology affirms, that twentieth-century ecumenism is connected with the decline of the West and 'a typical manifestation of the church in a secularized world'.

Not all the arguments about the ecumenical movement and the criticisms of the World Council of Churches carry real weight. Some have little substance, as they deal with administrative and technical problems which have partly been solved or are 'placed on the list' to be tackled. Some are not fair, as they do not take sufficiently into account the fact that all human institutions (the international organizations included) suffer from a 'sclerosis' of structures and from an inability to communicate effectively with a world-wide and local constituency. Some point to a number of shortcomings and mistakes of the Council which could eventually be corrected, but no creative alternative solutions are suggested. Raising again the question of this book, namely whether the World Council of Churches makes an authentic and singular contribution to the present world community, even the more pertinent criticisms and arguments, which I summarized under nine points, do not seem to penetrate deeply enough into the true nature and task of the Council and its constituent churches, except perhaps the last criticism.

According to my own judgment, the urgency and the challenge of the dialogue with other religions and ideologies has not been sufficiently communicated and evaluated. The very fact that the Council's Programme on 'Dialogue with People of Living Faiths and Ideologies' is comprised in a small sub-unit within Unit I (it was formerly a department within the Division of World Mission and Evangelism) is quite revealing. The aim of this Unit has been formulated as follows: 'To seek God's will for the unity of the church, to assist the churches to explore the content and meaning of the Gospel for their faith and mission, to encourage dialogue with men of other faiths and ideologies, and to enquire into the bearing of Christian belief on the spiritual and ethical issues posed for society by science and technology.' Following the thread of our inquiry, one is inclined to ask why the dialogue with other religions, and particularly with ideologies, has been classified within Unit I (Faith and Witness), and not in Unit II (Justice and Service), whose tasks I described in the previous chapter, or even in Unit III (Communication and Education). Dialogue in the midst of concerns such as Christian faith, witness and Christian social ethics is not given much room for movement. It is certainly not surprising that any book on the World Council of Churches has devoted proportionally only a few pages to the dialogue to which I wish to turn in the next two chapters.

V

The Dialogue with People of Living Faiths

In the light of the convictions and conclusions of the Second Vatican Council, Pope Paul VI established in Rome in 1964 the Secretariat for Non-Christians, entrusting it with the task of reappraising and fostering relations with non-Christian religions. The next year the Secretariat for Non-Believers was created by the Pope in order to co-ordinate spiritual and pastoral efforts for understanding the phenomenon of atheism based on scientific research into its historical-doctrinal, sociological and psychological perspectives. Both secretariats immediately went to work, sponsored a few consultations of Christian experts, and continue to publish an occasional bulletin in the field of their respective responsibilities. At the beginning plans were made for initiating dialogues with devotees of other religions and representatives of atheist conviction, but no contacts outside the walls of the church have been made or will be made in the near future. Although the two Secretariats continue their efforts to work in the spirit of *aggiornamento* of Vatican II, it has become quite clear that they are neither a real challenge to the Roman Catholic Church nor a sincere 'outstretched hand' to the multi-religious and secular world. The Secretariat for Non-Christians remains primarily concerned with information and research in the field of comparative religions. Likewise, the Secretariat for Non-Believers has no other choice than to analyse more profoundly modern atheism in its various forms, postponing the actual promotion of dialogue. The staff of both secretariats have little room for manoeuvre, and their activities are carefully controlled.

Particularly alarming is the fact that the name of each secretariat, in spite of the misgivings of several of its members and consultants, has still not been changed. The word 'non', it was rightly argued, has a pejorative and condescending connotation. It implies that religions other than the Christian religion, and secular systems of thought, are by their very nature and content inferior to Christianity. Their inspirations and standards of values have no ultimate significance as long as they are not corrected by the church's wisdom. Those who pronounce the 'no' have the right to question all other endeavours and to judge the truth which is not based on Christian revelation. Apparently the church still does not hear the voices of 'non-believers' and 'non-Christians' in the East and in the South rejecting centuries-old Christian spiritual paternalism and opposing a continuing Western urge for expansion or a monolithic ecclesiological approach to their 'heathen' world. They do not want to be 'saved' by being brought into the established institutional church which still claims to occupy the centre of world history. Such a church has to be watched both for its cultural and psychological egocentricity and self-defensiveness and for its missionary aggressiveness.

It took a long time before the word 'non' was dropped in the ecumenical movement. The phrase 'dialogue with people of living faiths and ideologies' became a standard expression in the World Council of Churches' vocabulary only five years ago. The change in terminology can be considered as a step forward. First of all, the use of the word 'dialogue' implies that Christians have become conscious of the fact that in the present pluralistic world nobody possesses an inherently privileged status over against others. Dialogue is the only appropriate form of living together; any relationship less than dialogue is monologue. Dialogue requires two *equal* partners and demands openness, honesty, humility and trust on both sides. Finally, no dialogue can take place without honest self-criticism and the willingness to change. The term 'people of living faiths' (the word 'men', used in the beginning, was replaced by the word 'people') implies that Christians want to meet *human beings* like themselves who are just as entitled as Christians to proclaim an authentic and existential faith in God and can claim to know something about the origin, purpose and destination of his universe. I will refer to the implications of the two words 'and ideologies' in the next chapter.

Before and after Uppsala, 1968

Of course, the understanding of non-Christian religions has been a long-standing concern in the ecumenical movement. As Islam continued to make headway in Africa and the Middle East, and Hinduism in India and Buddhism in various parts of Asia, the International Missionary Council explored ways of re-approaching and re-evaluating these and other religions. The International Conference at Jerusalem in 1928 spoke of 'values' in other religious faiths in a way which foreshadowed the Vatican II Declaration on the Relationships of the Church to Non-Christian Religions. The Tambaram Conference in 1938 expounded the implications of the church's evangelistic approach to other religions. Although the problem of the relationship between witness and dialogue was not completely lost in the central study process of the World Council of Churches, more attention was devoted to the whole problem only during the sixties.

The real impetus to grapple anew with this question came from Asia. The First Assembly of the East Asia Christian Conference in 1959 issued a report on 'New Steps in Asia in the Study of the Word of God and the Living Faiths of Men', which suggested that more attention be given to the interaction between religious beliefs and social changes. The Second Assembly of the East Asia Christian Conference in 1964 recommended to the churches a statement 'Christian Encounter with Men of Other Beliefs', and urged Christians to enter into a true conversation with men of other faiths, whether religious or not. The Assembly of the World Council's Commission on World Mission and Evangelism in Mexico City in 1963 expressed the hope that through the work of various Study Centres and through actual dialogue with people of other faiths, fresh insights might be gained which could enable an ongoing study on the 'Living Faiths' to enter a new phase, breaking through the stalemate of the debate which had been carried on in rather abstract terms since Tambaram.

The concept 'dialogue' was given real substance for the first time at a Consultation on 'Christian Dialogue with Men of Other Faiths', held at Kandy, Ceylon, in 1967, sponsored by the World Council of Churches. At Kandy Roman Catholic scholars also joined in the ecumenical debate for the first time. The statement of this consultation produced some exciting new insights into the theme of dialogue, and went considerably further than previous pronouncements of World Council meetings. The Kandy Consultation tried to face seriously the modern world of cultural and religious pluralism, evaluating new dimensions of multi-religious societies emerging in many countries in Asia and Africa. The following part of the statement could still serve as a good working definition of dialogue: 'Dialogue means a positive effort to attain a deeper understanding of the truth through mutual awareness of one another's convictions and witness. It involves an expectation of something new happening – the opening of a new dimension of which one was not aware before. Dialogue implies a readiness to be changed as well as to influence others. Good dialogue develops when one partner speaks in such a way that the other feels drawn to listen, and likewise when one listens so that the other is drawn to speak.'

The 1967 Consultation clearly recognized that 'there is far too much Christian communalism and ghettoism in both West and East', that many Christians are still satisfied with polite and voluntary co-existence, lacking a joyful and responsible awareness of 'human solidarity with all fellow-men, no matter what their colour, culture, faith or unbelief'. The observation that 'true dialogue is a progressive and cumulative process, which does not only take place through verbal communication, but through the dynamic contact of life with life', also marks the Kandy meeting as a significant step forward in the ecumenical movement. Unfortunately, the Consultation had little impact on the Council's Fourth Assembly at Uppsala. Though the term dialogue was used twenty-six times in the official Report, the word referred mostly to inter-confessional dialogue, particularly to the last two years' continuing conversations between the World Council and the Roman Catholic Church. The reactions to the Council's Programme on Dialogue with People of Living Faiths within subsequent Central Committee meetings have not been very positive. I will refer to these reactions in a moment.

Held at Ajaltoun, Lebanon, in 1970, a Consultation on 'Dialogue between Men of Living Faiths' for the first time brought together under the auspices of the World Council members of four living faiths: Hindus, Buddhists, Christians and Muslims. The emphasis of the conversations was primarily on the experience of dialogue itself, rather than on academic discussion about its nature and purpose. Questions of inter-religious dialogue on man and his temporal and ultimate destiny in the context of the struggle for world community and increasing inter-religious contacts were explored.

A few months later a Consultation at Zürich evaluated the Ajaltoun Consultation, considering some of the specific issues which Christians face in dialogue with men of other faiths and producing a notable *aide-mémoire*. Exploring again the relationship between dialogue and mission, the Consultation stated in its document that 'there is an understanding of mission which neither betrays the commitment of the Christians nor exploits the confidence and the reality of men of other faiths'. The same document placed the question of syncretism rightly in the context of indigenization. Christians need dialogue to enable them 'to find out both what are the authentic changes which the Gospel demands and the authentic embodiment which the Gospel offers'. The last paragraph of the *aide-mémoire* stressed anew the urgency of dialogue between Christians and people of other commitments. 'Christians must surely show great boldness in exploring ways forward to community, communication and communion between men at both the local and the world level. All the circumstances of human life on the globe at this present stage force upon us the search for a world community in which men can share and act together.'

The Commission on World Mission and Evangelism, meeting at Bangkok, Thailand, in January 1973, again pointedly expressed its concern for dialogue with people of living faiths. Much discussion was based on the Kandy statement and the Zürich *aide-mémoire*. Once more Christians were called to work with Muslims, Hindus, Buddhists, Jews and others 'to meet human needs, relieve human suffering, establish social justice, work for wider community and struggle for peace ...; as the interdependence between people and nations is increasing, there is a manifest need for world community.' Of course, in listening to one another, differences of opinion and approach are to be faced. Some of these differences may be resolved as partners in the dialogue learn to understand the mutual spiritual, experiential and conceptual background from which each side starts. 'As to apparently irreconcilable differences', Christians should remember their 'Lord's promise that the Spirit will lead them into all truth (John 16.13)'. Christian mission, the gathering at Bangkok stated, 'may once more become acceptable as an authentic expression of Christian faith and not be open to the charge of religious imperialism'.

Looking ahead into the near future, the Sub-Unit on Dialogue with People of Living Faiths hopes to sponsor a Consultation on Primal Religions, including the traditional religions of Africa, the religions in the Pacific area and tribal religions, all of which in some way or other are coming into touch with forces of modernization and secularization. Another multi-lateral type of dialogue similar to the one held at Ajaltoun in 1970, possibly also including Jews, will eventually be prepared. If the Council's Fifth Assembly takes place in Djakarta, Indonesia, a country where the great majority of people profess the Muslim faith, the concern for dialogue should make a substantial contribution to the style and content of the Assembly. The search for a wider community would, in fact, become an even clearer priority.

Orthodox Contributions

Orthodox theologians and church groups have made a specific and valuable contribution to the ongoing discussions and dialogue with people of other faiths. Metropolitan Georg Khodr, for instance, made a highly challenging and controversial presentation to the Central Committee, meeting at Addis Ababa in 1971. In his address, 'Christianity in a Pluralistic World – the Work of the Holy Spirit', he did not hesitate to say that 'Christ is everywhere hidden in the mystery of his lowliness. Any interpretation of religions is an interpretation in him. It is Christ alone who is received as light when grace visits a Brahman, a Buddhist or a Moslem reading their own scriptures.' Catholicism and Protestantism seem to have forgotten that the outpouring of the Holy Spirit on all flesh is not subordinated to the second person of the Trinity, but remains an ultimate prerogative of the Father. The gift of the Holy Spirit to the Gentiles is not a prolongation of the Incarnation, as the Spirit operates according to its own economy, making Christ present among all nations.

According to Orthodox teaching, Metropolitan Khodr asserted, the doctrine of creation includes the activity of the Holy Spirit from the very beginning, leading all men and all things in the course of world history to their ultimate fulfilment. The freedom of God cannot be limited to his providential and redemptive action revealed in some event of salvation history. Going beyond the idea of salvation history, we should find anew the meaning of the *oikonomia* of God, read all the other signs which he has erected outside the People of the Covenant, and investigate the authentic spiritual life of the non-baptized. God's dialogue with all mankind, Metropolitan Khodr pointed out, continues after the creation in so far as the cosmic covenant with Noah remains valid independently of the Abrahamic covenant. Israel is saved figuratively as the representative of humanity. Also, the New Israel keeps its mediatorial role, but God still continues to raise up other voices and vocations outside the confines of the Christian church.

Father Paul Verghese, Principal of the Orthodox Theological Seminary in Kerala, India, has been one of the most able and articulate advocates of the dialogue with people of other faiths. He has played a key role in the drafting of various World Council documents, and has written a number of searching essays on the theme of dialogue. A basic error of Christians, according to him, lies in 'the attempt to limit grace to the dispensation of the Incarnation in Jesus Christ. God has always been gracious; even the creation is an act of grace. Without that grace the creation would have immediately gone back to nothingness.' It is also wrong to cut the Holy Spirit off from influence outside the church. This is to deny that he is the agent of creation who is maker and creator of all things, leading towards their fulfilment. If the activity of the Holy Spirit in creation is not seen from the very beginning, 'the doctrine of the Holy Spirit will be egotistic, ecclesiologically exclusive and therefore sinful'. Father Verghese is further suspicious of those Christians who claim that they know all that has been revealed by God and arrogantly use their obviously limited understanding of God as a norm by which to evaluate other religions in which, according to them, the little truth is mixed up with so much error that the truth becomes insignificant. 'If we are honest and secure enough, we could grant that our apprehension of the Christian revelation itself is woefully imperfect, and that that very apprehension may be significantly altered by our knowledge of other religions.' Coming to terms intellectually and spiritually with his fellow human beings in India and elsewhere, he writes: 'I believe that mankind is one in ultimate essence, that my individuality in this time does not reveal my true being, until I identify myself in consciousness with all humanity in all places and at all times. The corporate nature of humanity is a fundamental axiom in my understanding of reality.' At the same time he confesses unashamedly that he is a Christian and that being a baptized member of a community of faith which believes that it is the Body of Christ does make a real difference.

'The Precarious Vision'

There is little doubt that the World Council's Sub-Unit on Dialogue with People of Living Faiths and Ideologies has made tremendous progress and continues to function effectively. It indeed speaks a new language, and its new concerns are shared by other World Council units and individual Christians within the Council's constituency. There is now a firm conviction that *living* in dialogue must frequently precede theological reflection on dialogue in an exclusively Christian context. The conversations in multi-cultural communities on international and local levels should continue, and churches are invited to participate in these ventures. There should also be a positive response to initiatives for dialogue from men of other faiths, and a selective participation in world religious meetings. At the same time, several Third World Ecumenical Study Centres continue to perform their pioneering task, living and working on and across the frontiers of Christian communities. Some of these important and active centres are: The Christian Institute for the Study of Religion and Society in Jaffna, Ceylon; the Christian Institute for the Study of Religion and Society in Bangalore, India; the Christian Study Centre on Chinese Religion and Culture in Hongkong; the Christian Institute for the Study of Religion and Society in Singapore; and several other centres in Cuba, Uruguay, Mexico, Nigeria, Cameroun, Ghana, Kenya, Morocco, the Near East and Pakistan. All these centres have provided meeting points between Christians and representatives of other faiths and are in touch with various aspects of a given society and culture on a basis of study and mutual give and take.

Yet true dialogue has been and still is a concern of a few thousand individuals actively engaged in promoting deeper discussions and searching for areas of mutual understanding and co-operation. Most churches and Christians are uninformed about the events of this last decade, or take a neutral (more frequently even a hostile) stand with regard to the possibilities and results of the current dialogue. The Council's Programme on Dialogue with People of Living Faiths has already been met with reservations and criticisms within the Central Committee itself. Several members of this Committee are not involved in a life of community together with men of living faiths, and have no actual experience of conversing regularly with people of other persuasions. It is not surprising, therefore, that they either dialogue among themselves about the possibility of dialogue or are worried that dialogue will weaken mission and lead to syncretism. If any dialogue should take place, its goal must be that of making 'strangers into fellow-citizens in the household of God'. It is added that, after all, the gospel has not been preached and received in dialogue form. For others, any dialogue presupposes that Christianity is one religion among many. This cannot be accepted, as Christians will be in danger of losing their identity. These and other arguments indicate that several of the churches' delegates to the Central Committee have great difficulty in recognizing that 'dialogue is one of the crucial areas of relationships between Christians and men of other faiths today' and that theological reflection on this dialogue 'must continue, not in the isolation of academic discussions', but in the midst of life together in the very same community.

In other gatherings, too, such as the World Council's Assembly at Uppsala, uncertainty about the nature and function of dialogue exists. In the Report *Renewal in Mission*, adopted by the Assembly, we read: 'As Christians we believe that Christ speaks in the dialogue ... Dialogue and proclamation are not the same. The one complements the other in a total witness. But sometimes Christians are not able to engage either in open dialogue or proclamation. Witness is then a silent one of living the Christian life and suffering for Christ.' Here again the question of dialogue is exclusively discussed in relation to the question of mission, evangelism and witness. Christ must speak in all circumstances in each dialogue, otherwise the dialogue is not genuine. Does the church's commission, one is tempted to ask, only consist of bringing Christ to a 'Christ-less world'? Must witness always have priority over

the dialogue between the church and the world? Cannot
Christians, by *'being* in a dialogue', without witnessing and
preaching, communicate in a real and genuine sense with persons of other faiths or ideologies? On the other hand, admitting
that witness and dialogue are not opposed notions, are the
Christians who drafted the statement cited above really conscious of the fact that all other human beings also witness from
the heart of their existence to ultimate concerns expressed in
their words and actions? Why should Christians enjoy the
privilege of first expressing the concerns of *their* faith and
then hearing the other's witness? Christians are right to believe that Christ is present in every dialogue. But they do not
seem to serve Christ's cause if they feel compelled to introduce
his name each time before the dialogue has really started.

One can well imagine situations in which it is not useful
for Christians to engage in proclamation. But that Christians
should refuse to participate in open dialogue and instead prefer
to witness by silently living the Christian life sounds unreal,
and corresponds to the isolated existence in 'Christian communalism and ghettoism', mentioned in the Kandy declaration.
Quiet suffering for Christ without being related to either
proclamation or dialogue is no real option at all. Christians
only suffer for their Master when they dare to introduce his
name or when they are willing *to be* a person in the conversation with other persons who do not believe in him.

Finally, the expression 'total witness' also seems unfortunate
and misplaced. Is it not an overstatement to say that a Christian in the act of proclamation functions as a total witness?
Christians should know that the real outcome of every
evangelistic campaign is exclusively the work of the Spirit.
They should not speak, therefore, of total witness in the realm
of inter-religious or inter-humanistic dialogue. Christians who
are not absolutely sure of their faith and sometimes little at
ease in their church above all need to engage in dialogue to
hear the critical viewpoints of, for instance, an avowed atheist,
and so be strengthened in their faith and service for Christ.
Their witness is then not a *conditio sine qua non* for dialogue,

but an unexpected result of one or several dialogues. Conversely, it is not true that total conversion corresponds to total witness. The other person in the dialogue is never a person to be converted on the spot. An incredible and unacceptable message would simply violate and crush his own inner conviction. Any real faith or insight grows slowly in a long process of communication.

These few examples of opposition to dialogue, misunderstanding or manipulation of dialogue show that the World Council of Churches' task of communication and persuasion is a long and difficult one. Despite the high quality and the clarity of the Kandy statement, the Zürich *aide-mémoire* and the Bangkok 1973 Section on Dialogue with People of Living Faiths, and despite other pronouncements inviting the Council's member churches to share with adherents to other creeds and philosophies a common humanity and a common concern for material and spiritual enrichment of that humanity, for the majority of Christians the whole matter of dialogue remains a strange phenomenon. They still cannot grasp that they have much more in common with many peoples of other faiths or unbelief, a fact which was not yet anticipated during the first half of this century. Living in their self-contained Christian community, they consider dialogue with representatives of other communities as a curious kind of activity of some extroverted Christians believing in a greater inter-dependence of the human race. If any dialogue should take place at all, they feel it better that only 'notes' on matters of religious tradition, doctrine and worship should be 'compared', in line with a policy of polite but not binding co-existence.

Summarizing the content of this chapter, one can conclude that, in most situations in which it finds itself, the Christian church is not yet ready to meet and to receive Jews, Muslims, Buddhists, Hindus and peoples of other religious convictions as equal partners in bi-lateral and multi-lateral dialogues. The church, claiming to be a unique force in history, cannot really 'step down' to the level of equality with other religious communities, except for its world-wide humanitarian services. Nor is it aware that the eventual sharing of common beliefs and common purposes with other religions is not only of significance to the religious part of mankind but can also contribute to the building of a greater world community of *all* men and women. In other words, by not recognizing other religious families as constituent parts of a world civilization, the church has even more difficulty in accepting secular and ideological communities as necessary components of a world community. For that reason it hardly struggles to understand and to evaluate itself as a community among other communities (secular communities included) and to find its appropriate place in the universal community of communities. Continuing to affirm first of all its identity as a community *set apart from* other communities, instead of continually finding its identity as a peculiar community *in the midst of* other communities, the church lags behind in the ecumenical movement.

A final remark. The World Council's Programme on Dialogue with People of Living Faiths is quite aware of the limitations of all dialogue. It knows through experience that dialogue is never more than a conversation between *human* beings and cannot indefinitely transcend the limitations of their *human* ideologies, religions and visions. Even if devotees of different religions together reach new sights and a more profound understanding of man's existence in nature and society, the most meaningful dialogue cannot lead them beyond their human possibilities and failures. As a part of their common language will remain ambiguous, and common action will always be coloured by a selfish desire for security and peace, an unlimited confidence in dialogue must end in disillusion and frustration. Precisely because the World Council of Churches is conscious of these limitations to dialogue, it is clearly ahead of its constituency and deserves a much wider support which is difficult to foresee in the near future. Thus its valuable and specific contribution to the search for a world community within the realm of inter-religious dialogue is so far a marginal and minimal one.

VI

'. . . and Ideologies'

The Christian Aversion to Atheism

Christians attending the World Missionary Conference at Edinburgh in 1910 still believed that potentially the whole world could be Christianized if only all missionary forces were combined and an all-out effort to preach the gospel to all nations were made. They realized, of course, that some serious obstacles had to be faced. Speakers at Edinburgh mentioned 'harmful external influences', such as 'literature of indecent or, more commonly, of agnostic and atheistic character', which defends 'materialistic views and extreme evolutionary positions' and attacks Christianity with boldness. Other dangers are the increasing use of foreign liquors, new forms of gambling, the importation of prostitutes and the immoral life of members of foreign communities. Such a bad representation of Western civilization to the heathen world cannot be tolerated if the church wants to overcome hostile influences and permeate new world movements with the spirit of Christ. 'Only the religion commended by the most convincing examples in dominating individual and social life and commercial and international relations will be earnestly sought after and permanently accepted.'

It is exceedingly important, the Conference at Edinburgh warned, that missionary colleges and schools should hold strictly to the policy pursued in the past of insisting that students attending these institutions should accept the religious instruction provided. Missionaries should not be allowed to learn first from the hostile camp promoting rationalistic, atheistic and socialistic literature of all kinds. Western education in Europe and America should reiterate its 'old moral teaching', 'hasten to preoccupy the ground' and guide all Christians past 'the pitfalls which unbelieving literature has strewn'. Edinburgh 1910, which has long been recognized as the beginning of the twentieth-century ecumenical movement, was convinced that the challenge of the non-Christian world provides the Christian faith with the vision and the power that are essential for the basic solution of the world's problems.

Obviously, the church has undergone significant changes during the first half of this century. No Christian still dreams today that an all-out evangelistic movement on six continents will convert many millions of agnostic and atheist human beings to Christianity. The church today finds itself in a minority position, and it is very unlikely that that position will be changed in the next decades. Yet, examining the church's attitude towards modern expressions of atheism and particularly towards anti-religious or atheistic ideologies, one wonders whether after sixty years of ecumenical movement the church today substantially differs from the church at the beginning of this century.

Christians, particularly in the West, still abhor atheism as an impossible possibility of looking at the world and dealing with human problems. Atheism is a dangerous vacuum which has to be filled immediately and by all means with some kind of theism. Atheism cannot be seen otherwise than as an utter denial and opposition to theism, striving only to eradicate any trace of religion. Whether theoretical or practical, atheism starts from an 'immoral' or 'sub-human' understanding of man. There must be, therefore, something basically wrong in the mind and spirit of atheist humanists and communists; their theories and suggestions for radical reform of society cannot aim at anything positive. Until they are converted to Christianity or another religion, their behaviour has to be seriously questioned and their actions carefully checked.

The story of primitive anti-communism and anti-communist crusades in the Christian church is a long and sad one. Many hundreds of books, pamphlets and articles have been written by church leaders and Christian laymen on 'how to resist and to fight communism', this godless and insane ideology terrorizing and enslaving millions of people around the world. Pope Pius XI referred in his Encyclical Letter, *Divini Redemptoris* (1937), to 'the immortal Leo XIII', who defined communism as 'the fatal plague which insinuates itself into the very marrow of human society only to bring about its ruin' and himself added: 'Communism is intrinsically wrong, and no one who would save Christian civilization may collaborate with it in any undertaking whatsoever.'

Even today, a great number of Christians facing the communist world do not question for a moment their 'superior' wisdom and better insight into human nature and world affairs. They do not wish to make an attempt to understand the honest and deep-rooted anti-religious feelings of millions of militant communists, who cannot believe any longer that the Christian churches are engaged in the struggle for social and economic justice. Even those who admit that Marxists at some point rightly criticized Christian civilization are convinced that now, having learned a few good lessons and corrected some mistakes in Western liberal society, they are outside the reach of their attacks and can continue to live on their own behalf. Is there indeed a great difference between being upset and condemning 'indecent, materialistic and atheistic literature' sixty years ago, and not accepting today without reservation the communist as a fully human being with equal rights and equal concerns in the present international society? What Christian message today has replaced the Edinburgh 1910 message advising the church to reiterate its 'old moral teaching' and 'to hasten to preoccupy the ground'?

In comparison to the flood of anti-communist literature, good informative and educational material on 'how to encounter anti-communism' in church circles is rare. Within the ecumenical movement of the last few decades one is not even

aware of this fact. The World Council itself has twice published a leaflet entitled *Questions and Answers about the
World Council of Churches and Communism*, trying to ward
off accusations of being a communist-infiltrated organization
and to correct some basic misunderstandings about the Council's stand on Marxist ideology. These leaflets have little
educational value and hardly appease the conscience of many
Christians who still condemn communism as violently as Pope
Pius XI. The very few books dealing adequately with the
phenomenon of anti-communism are now out-of-date.

The church's very real problem of how to face atheism
honestly and how to deal earnestly with an atheistic ideology
does, of course, go beyond the problem of limiting the irres-
ponsibility and damage of its primitive anti-communism. In
connection with the previous chapter we must ask what
contributions the World Council has made to the so-called
Christian-Marxist dialogue in the sixties, which took place
mainly in Western Europe and in a few cities in the USA, and
how the Council has approached the whole question of
ideology and ideologies. As will be seen, the World Council
made very little direct contribution to an actual dialogue
with Marxists, considering the encounter more a burden than
a challenge. The great difficulty of finding not only European
Marxists, but also Marxists from the Third World willing to
participate in a new and genuine dialogue which distinguishes
itself to some extent from the initial dialogue in the last
decade, has been used several times recently as an excuse for
the absence of a clearer mind and a deeper understanding of
the problem of atheism and ideology.

The World Council and the Problem of Ideology

At the First Assembly in Amsterdam in 1948, Christian
churches were admonished 'to reject the ideologies of both
Communism and *laissez-faire* capitalism', seeking 'to draw men
away from the false assumption that these extremes are the
only alternatives'. The same Assembly stated further that 'it
is the responsibility of Christians to seek new, creative solu-

tions which never allow either freedom (in the Western hemisphere) or justice (in Eastern society) to destroy the other'. No attempt was made, however, to describe in any detail what new and creative alternatives could be offered and in what kind of socio-political framework they could be realized. The 'Second Statement on the Issues in the Study of Rapid Social Change', published by the Council's Department on Church and Society in 1956, did not shed more light on the matter. We read in this statement: 'It is a big problem for Christians in a time of great change *to avoid* a "Christian" social ideology, expressing in a *too definite and universal way* what is the meaning of Christian justice and freedom' (italics mine). The fear and embarrassment at formulating in some way the churches' stand on contemporary ideological issues is clearly expressed.

Looking at the documents of the Second Vatican Council one is not surprised that with reference to 'ideology' they too yield only one rather unrelated and naïve sentence referring to the problem of ideological propaganda: 'If an economic order is to be created which is genuine and universal, there must be an abolition of excessive desire for profit, nationalistic pretentions, the lust for political domination, militaristic thinking and intrigues designed to spread and impose ideologies.' Reacting to such a typically religious, but, in the realm of the socio-economic sciences, almost meaningless statement, one immediately asks which model of a genuine and universal economic order is envisaged, and how one goes about abolishing effectively all those aggressive and malicious human attitudes.

It was only at the World Conference on Church and Society in Geneva in 1966 that a need was felt to explore further 'the relation between the structures of Christian thought and the various other combinations of theoretical analysis and strategy for social action, sometimes known as ideologies.' Conference participants openly spoke out and admitted that 'there is no agreement among Christians themselves on the degree to which analysis and action in Christian ethics itself must wrestle with ideological bias'. Although no recommendation was made to engage in a systematic or more profound study of the relationships between Christian social theology and secular ideology, the Conference urged the World Council of Churches to initiate an informal dialogue with Marxists, for the furtherance of peace and progress for all mankind. A Christian-Marxist dialogue, under the auspices of the Department on Church and Society, took place at Geneva in 1968, concerning itself with problems of 'Humanization of Technological and Economic Development in the Industrialized Countries and in the Third World'. A small steering committee of Christians and Marxists, which had prepared the Geneva conference, met again in 1969 to prepare for an eventual continuation of the dialogue, but no further conversations have taken place since the meeting in 1968.

In 1970 the Department on Church and Society organized an exploratory conference on the subject 'Technology and the Future of Man and Society'. Among several topics the implications of the present ideological struggle were debated. It is interesting to note that the same preoccupation of the Church and Society Conference in 1966 with the problem 'to what extent Christian ethics must wrestle itself with ideological bias', was introduced again in this exploratory conference. Once more it was clearly stated that there is no agreement 'on the degree to which theology should risk becoming ideological in order to show man the way towards more responsible use of technological power and liberation of oppressive structures of it'. The Conference went on to say that 'the relation of faith to ideology remains a question to be worked out in concrete situations'. On the other hand, for the first time in the history of ecumenical social thought, it was plainly admitted that 'theology is always ideological as it expresses itself in a particular context', and that 'this is in one sense the virtue of theology' because 'the Word of God must become concrete in particular times and places'. At the end of this chapter of the Report, it is noted once more, as in previous conferences, that the dialogue with Marxism, 'the most important single ideology' attempting 'to restructure technological

power in a new and radical way, is central for Christian responsibility in building the future of man'. This impressive
phrase remained empty, however, as no new contacts with
Marxists were sought.

Finally, the Working Committee on Church and Society
meeting in Nemi, Italy, in 1971, to plan the next steps in the
ecumenical enquiry on the 'Future of Man and Society in a
World of Science-Based Technology', compiled in its Third
Report, entitled 'Images of the Future', a list of current
ideologies describing very briefly : (1) liberal ideology; (2) Marxist ideology; (3) social democratic ideology; (4) technocratism;
(5) nationalism; (6) reactive ideologies; and (7) cultural tradi-
tionalism, adding to each characterization in a few sentences
a critical evaluation and a healing vision of their future. Although the attempt to give an equal number of bad marks to
each ideology and to suggest a few cures for every ideology's
ills might seem to stem from a magnanimous (ecumenical)
mind and even to follow an objective method of sociological
enquiry, the whole descriptive catalogue of current ideologies
is a useless instrument providing no challenge or inspiration
for specific political actions in actual power conflicts and social
struggles.

The Department on Church and Society was obviously not
very interested in following up the valid suggestion of the
1970 exploratory conference that the relation between faith
and ideology in concrete situations should be worked out and
that there should be more exploration in depth of the degree
to which theology should risk becoming clearly ideological in
order to indicate to individuals and peoples ways of liberating
themselves from oppressive political and socio-economic systems, and building a responsibly affluent, more equal, just and
human society. Only one participant remarked that the Nemi
report 'was going up a blind alley' and that utopias are needed
'projected by adventurous ideologues on the basis of convincing
analysis of present trends and leading to actions that engage
us fully in their realization. We need pictures of how human
community might be structured so as to be peaceful, hopeful

and loving, pictures which convince us by realistic analysis that we could get from here to there.'

As the concern for a deeper analysis and a better understanding of the problem of ideology had to be inserted somewhere and somewhat more officially into the World Council's programme, the Central Committee meeting at Addis Ababa in 1971 decided to add the two words 'and ideologies' to the phrase 'Dialogue with People of Other Living Faiths'. No suggestions or recommendations were made as to how to work out a combined dialogue with religions and ideologies. The majority of the Central Committee had little idea how to create contacts with humanists, Marxists and atheists and how to prepare for a meaningful conversation. They only decided to classify secular ideologies together with world religions and suggested that dialogue with men of different ideologies should take place within a wide religious framework. While it is right not to put ideologies in an entirely different category by themselves, because religions in dialogue are apt to defend their common 'religious front' against a threatening secular world, and because all religions tend to deny vigorously any ideological infiltration or bias within their own systems of belief, the Addis Ababa mandate nevertheless diverted attention from the necessity of dealing with the problem of ideology from all angles.

There is little doubt that the Christian 'allergy to atheism', to which I referred in the beginning of this chapter, still plays a role in the World Council's vacillation and hesitation to face the whole issue of ideology squarely. Atheist systems of theory and action must be kept at a distance and cannot be given the honour of a thorough investigation. At the most, Christianity can eventually be in 'dialogue' with secular ideologies, keeping well in mind that they frequently turn into a substitute or even a fully-fledged religion. A secular ideology sometimes takes the place of a secular faith in order to respond to man's ever-present religious needs. If this happens, it is rather easy for Christians to denounce its absurd religious claims and to ridicule its utopia of a classless society in which all human misery and alienation are totally eliminated. Christians cannot fall into this trap of idolatry because they always have recourse to their own transcendental wisdom. But since this kind of 'dialogue' will hardly lead anywhere, it also seems to make little sense that they should be in the forefront of the discussion on the nature and implications of ideology. Is it not true, after all, that Christianity is not an ideology and has nothing to do with ideology?

Christianity is not an Ideology

The World Council of Churches has indeed been of this opinion when on several occasions it has affirmed that the gospel transcends all economic ideologies and that the acknowledgment of the Lordship of Christ challenges the inevitable tendency of the human race to give particular patterns of economic organization a religious sanction which they do not deserve. The lack of the knowledge of God as the judge of history is at the root of all ideological and totalitarian triumphalism in any part of the world. The proclamation of the Word of God, with a profound sense of its relevance to political and ideological conflicts, remains the central task of the churches subscribing to the aims of the ecumenical movement. Moreover, competent theologians, bent over the problem of the relationship of theology and ideology, have insisted over and over again that it is the 'subject and object' of the Christian faith, namely God's grace, which prevents Christianity being turned into an ideology. Christianity cannot be approached and grasped on the same level as ideology simply because the horizons of its declaration of faith do not coincide with the daily apprehension of factual reality and the experience of the empirical natural and social sciences.

There are other reasons why Christianity and ideology should not be placed on the same level of knowledge and action. Christian faith is the acceptance of a vocation and not the deduction of an interpretation. Faith never turns into sight; it is always eschatological, otherwise it would cease to be faith. Faith as an experience of a transcendent God makes every

ideology transcendent by its own transcendental necessity in
so far as ideology turns a limited area of tangible and inner-
worldly experience into an absolute. It is precisely the task of
the church to warn ideologies not to yield to the temptation
of becoming a faith, replacing analysis with creed, or principles
by a message, but to remain a means of providing rational
historical interpretations and initiatives for change.

It is hardly surprising that the Department on Church and
Society, in line with this correct but one-sided argument about
the incompatibility of theology with ideology, has never
manifested an eagerness to clarify and to update an 'ecumenical' concept of ideology and to engage in a serious study of the
deliberate or unconscious ideological presuppositions implied
in the formulation and implementation of a number of World
Council programmes. It has conceived of its task primarily in
terms of criticizing liberal and revolutionary ideologies in
order to liberate ecumenical social theology from ideological
freight. In speaking of the modern confusion of 'ideological
tongues' and stripping 'technological humanism', with its roots
in the liberal Western tradition, and 'revolutionary humanism',
as given classic form by Karl Marx, to the bones of error and
failure, the Department has given few concrete guidelines for
responsible political and social action. One is sometimes under
the impression that its peculiar dialectical reasoning and its
critical analysis of secular ideologies conveniently serve as a
defence of its own eclectic approach to problems of society
and as a pointer to the validity of the gospel which inspires
its programmes. Examining (sometimes quite penetratingly)
certain socio-economic problems, the Department need not
declare itself in a given situation in favour of, for instance, a
'moderate socialist' or a 'chastened and post-liberal democratic'
outlook, because it cannot identify itself with the failures and
the deadlock of ideologies which it questioned and outdistanced.

We arrive here at the crux of the problem of ideology in
the ecumenical movement. The word 'ideology' has been and
still is used almost exclusively in a negative and pejorative
sense, meaning an artificially created system of ideas or inter-

pretations of situations which are not the outcome of concrete experiences but a kind of distorted knowledge of them. Ideology, in other words, serves to cover up the real situation and works upon individuals as a kind of compulsion. This element of subjection to an ideology is particularly strong in the entire West – and also in the ecumenical movement – because the majority of people are fashioned by a traditional liberalism which, though an ideological system, has insistently refused to be classified as such. As ideology is always a function of a group and propagates the collective involvement of the masses in a given situation, ideology itself is rejected, since individualism is the very essence of liberal ideology. If ideology has after all infiltrated theology, then theology must be cleansed as much as possible from these totalitarian, destructive and inhuman ideological components.

There is, however, much evidence in the course of human history that not only are Christianity and ideology not systematically opposed, but that Christianity itself has turned into an ideology. Christians have far too often overlooked this fact. Becoming confused by the collective stimuli of a human group and eager to play a competitive role among secular institutions and movements, the church all too visibly and too frequently has replaced the kingdom of God by Christian civilization and the gospel by social principles of biblical religion. Whenever the church has mistaken its faith for an ideology – sometimes in a revolutionary manner, but mostly in a conservative and reactionary way – it has justified cultural, economic, social and political conditions which cannot claim permanent validity. The 'ideological contamination' of Christian ethics is not just a matter of degree, but reaches to the root of the church's involvement in any complicated matter of society. All the churches – confessional distinctions hardly play a role – are invaded by, and have to wrestle with, a whole range of potentially ideological problems such as nationalism, violent revolution, the consumer society, the search for native cultural roots, pacifism, racial power movements, deification of the state, development aid, technological advance and so on. These human and social concerns, sometimes turning into a hardened ideology, not only creep into the household of the church, but confront the people of God as they manifest themselves in the midst of any society. Some of these blurred or more explicit ideologies, but more particularly outspoken political ideologies like neo-capitalism, socialism, communism and totalitarianism also appear at the international level within the ecumenical movement. Although the World Council of Churches has managed rather skilfully to steer clear of the rocks of sharp ideological controversies, the pertinent question still remains whether or not ideological undercurrents have moved the ship into a particular direction and whether the course should not be changed.

If ecumenical Christianity is to have an impact on secular decision-making processes today and make its contribution to a growing world civilization, it is not enough that many Christians should readily admit that a number of churches support reactionary and totalitarian governments, defending these régimes in the name of Western Christian democracy. It is not even enough when the church as a whole repents for its persistent inclination more or less tacitly to favour the *status quo* of a seemingly not too oppressive or too exploitative bourgeois society. Christians should make it perfectly clear that the churches and their representatives are exposed to the same temptation to demonstrate power and prestige as any secular institution, organization or movement. In a recent study entitled *Ideology in the Church*, the German sociologist O. Schreuder mentions four sources from which 'Christian' ideological impulses can emerge: (1) The general need for validity and legitimacy of the total society and the special needs of single social groupings; (2) The social need religious institutions have for power; (3) The demands of ecclesiastical organizations and the self-interest of church officials; (4) The competitive relationships between religious communities.*

* O. Schreuder, *Ideologie in der Kirche*, Walter Verlag, Olten 1967, pp. 124-140.

Ideology in a Constructive Context

Can some steps be taken beyond the present uncertain and sometimes confusing situation in which the World Council of Churches finds itself? Can a creative and dialectical relationship between ideology and Christianity be worked out in actual concrete situations? I personally believe that this is possible and within the reach of the World Council's calling. I will try to outline in four points the new direction in which the ecumenical movement could be steered.

1. The ecumenical constituency could be gradually educated and convinced that the term 'ideology' can and should be used in a positive and pragmatic sense. Here I venture a few working definitions. Ideology is a coherent body of value-laden ideas that serves as a guide and impulse to action. Or: ideology is a theoretical and analytical structure of thought which undergirds successful action to realize revolutionary change in society or to justify the *status quo*. Perhaps the definition of Luis Alberto Gomez de Souza, a political scientist from Brazil, is even better: 'Ideology is a set of dynamics expressing the interests of social groups, with the purpose of preserving or changing the social structure.'* These working definitions imply that ideology, by simplifying complex social situations, offers many people from diverse backgrounds the possibility of explaining something of the latent meaning to be found in human history and of co-operating in the struggle to reach certain common goals. Moreover, an ideological system stresses the collective involvement of large groups of people in a given situation and the necessity of wide and active participation in the gradual process of social awakening and change.

Thus ideology as an integral part of contemporary society can provide an opportunity for self-understanding and serve as a dynamic factor in social change, in so far as it is a reality and will be directed by specific groups acting in accordance with carefully conceived plans. Without needing to rely on a

* In *Anticipation*, World Council of Churches Department on Church and Society, no. 2, June 1970, p. 15.

total programme and a world-view for their security, Christians can co-operate with others in efforts to work towards a greater intelligibility, and in this way to contribute to the well-being and unity of all men. Hence the conclusion is that ideology can help all men, including Christians, in achieving desirable social change, and sometimes facilitates undesirable social change.

2. Once we have defined ideology in this way, it becomes clear that theology is never a 'pure' discipline and can never be 'neutral'. Any kind of theology which tries to universalize all aspects of human life under its own ahistorical and idealistic categories has to be rejected. Ecumenical theology deals with the transformation and the unity of the world, and for that very reason is related to ideology, playing an important role in the ideological struggle. True faith compels Christians to face social and political realities and to participate in the struggle for human liberation and for the elimination of alienation, exploitation, segregation and for a just international society. Theology can thereby perform a crucial function by detecting ideological forces which principally defend the order of the *status quo* of society and do not promote any necessary change and progress. A greater part of mankind is still dominated by unconscious, and therefore mystifying and destructive, ideologies, which resist renewal and change in political and socio-economic structures and do not indicate any clear choice for urgent priorities in the historical process.

Theology can both create a new awareness of situations of injustice and oppression which contradict the gospel, and also attack a hidden ideological framework which holds a society together. Having denounced a traditional ideological infrastructure, and urged many Christians to step back from a given system, it can then encourage the breaking down of present structures of alienation and enslavement. Theology, however, further plays an equally important role by participating in the elaboration of a substitute ideology, which can create a new conscious and critical infrastructure of society and assure its slow but effective reconstruction and transfor-

mation. The only alternative to being enslaved by an unconscious ideological ethos is to tackle courageously the task of
producing the best ideology which can offer clues for the
understanding of man and history and the future prospects of
the human enterprise.

3. Christians have no reason to be afraid of examining the
actual links the churches maintain with the established political and economic powers and of asking the specific question:
what kind of relationships are really in accord with the
churches' message and mission? Christians know only too
well, but admit only on rare occasions, that the church,
whether through lack of vision or simply for fear of the
violence resulting from social disorder, still frequently accepts
the role of chief apologist or passive spectator of an unjust
social order. Interwoven into the complex fabric of relationships with economic and social powers, the churches enjoy
certain freedoms and benefits resulting from these actual
relations. By endorsing a given ideology they occupy a guaran-
teed place in the established order. It is essential, therefore,
that the churches examine as objectively as possible to what
extent their own institutional systems are infiltrated and mani-
pulated by surrounding ideological powers. There is still far
too little precise and penetrating information about the
churches' tacit adaptation or challenging response to liberal,
centrist or socialist ideologies.

This kind of examination and information is needed even
more urgently within the World Council of Churches. The
opportunity has been given, and should no longer be postponed,
of undertaking several studies of deliberate or unconscious
ideological presuppositions implicit in several World Council
programmes and policies. The Sub-Unit on Church and Society
concerned with the impact of accelerated scientific discoveries,
the explosive and unchecked development of technological
power and its application, the experimentation in the field of
genetics, the global threat to human environment, the responsible use of nature's resources, is involved in issues which are
all ideologically conditioned. Similarly, World Council pro-

grammes on Development, Racism, Aid, which I described
shortly in the third chapter, have several ideological components.

Furthermore, there is a real need to plan for some larger
World Council gatherings of theologians, church leaders and a
considerable number of Christian lay people from various
continents who would spell out and defend their ideological
allegiance or opposition to their national government and
express their concerns about the undiminished international
ideological hostility, provoked and fostered by big-power
nations and Third World countries alike. Such encounters
would at last help the Council to know much better – and
that knowledge is far from superfluous, but of great relevance
to many church matters – who really, at establishment or grass-
roots church levels, backs up or criticizes a 'Western', 'Eastern',
or 'Southern' ideology. Furthermore, during such gatherings
positions on liberal, pragmatic or evolutionary, and social
democratic ideologies, as well as on European and Asian communism, Latin American Marxism and African socialism,
could be formulated and stated. The last World Council's
statement on communism at the Evanston Assembly is not
only twenty years old, but also far too general and too much
a response to a very different international situation of bi-
lateral American-Russian tension.

4. Precisely within the World Council of Churches the concept of ideological pluralism could be cherished, I believe, and
an attempt be made to bring together opposing ideological
groups in order that they may speak to one another and work
with one another in creative tension. The question here is not
whether the ecumenical movement should be more political
and more to the right, the centre or the left, but whether the
world-wide church can create a well-co-ordinated forum providing opportunities for sharing insights and generating constructive criticisms across the whole range of ideological
experiences and options. Ideological debates can take place on
the basis of common Christian commitment and as an expression of mutual concern and support. During the Central Com-

mittee meetings at Utrecht, Holland, in August 1972, several
dialogues between 'moderate' and 'radical' groups took place
and it was 'proved' that the ecumenical fellowship to which
all are committed can comprehend various ideological encounters.

Undoubtedly, at other ecumenical gatherings efforts will and
should be made to win participants over to a more cautious or
a more revolutionary position, but this can only happen if
rigid dogmatic opinions are rejected, tendencies towards
intolerance of other options are unmasked and no short-cut
solutions are proposed by resorting to internal power politics.
An open working agenda on ideological problems which arises
out of the very nature of the ecumenical movement must be
provided. Further, the need for ideological tools in delibera-
tions and tasks must be recognized without singling out one
global social theory as a working hypothesis. Finally, these
ideological tools are to be chosen, modified and adapted in
relation to specific situations as well as to common world-wide
problems without requiring a total identification between
Christianity and any political ideology.

Perhaps these four points contain too much wishful thinking. Perhaps it will hardly be possible for the World Council
of Churches to change its unconscious ideological predicament
into a conscious one. Perhaps greater ideological clarity in its
own ranks would not much improve its position as a community living in the midst of and for the sake of secular communities. It is quite certain, however, that so far the Council
is as much confused as the churches on the issue of ideology
and ideologies and that it has few means of coming in contact
with more clearly defined ideological groups. It still tends to
forget that the *homo religiosus* and the *homo ideologicus* are
parts of the same human being and that the world-wide Christian community is critically watched by secular communities
for its ambiguous and deceiving unideological stand on political and socio-economic world issues. The secular world cannot
be blamed for being bewildered that the World Council is on
the one hand engaged in 'progressive' programmes of combat-

ing racism and furthering world development and on the other hand naïvely believes that a theme such as 'ideology as a secular *faith*' is an important and appropriate subject for discussion with Marxists. Is the World Council indeed open to all human persons and groups, does it generously contribute to the humanization of mankind, or is it caught in its self-contained organization and consequently not aware of imposing its 'ecumenical ideology' on the modern world?

VII

The Humanness and Identity
of the Institution

When we discussed 'ecumenical' aspects and dimensions of
Islam and Judaism and their respective contribution as religious communities to the world community very briefly in the
opening chapter, our evaluation of these religions did not turn
out to be very positive. Islam still has great difficulty in recognizing the equal status of other religious communities. Its ultimate goal remains the winning over or even the subduing of
the whole world to the Islamic faith. The domination of its
divine revelation must be established over all realms of life.
It has no other choice than to do battle and to proselytize.
Islam's desire to enter into dialogue with other religions is
minimal and its attitude towards the secular world and modern
ideological movements is often outspokenly hostile. The future
theocracy, to which the Qur'ān as unalterable and eternally
valid Holy Scripture refers, cannot be questioned and must be
realized.

Judaism continues to suffer from the alternative of believing
that it is the only elect people to fulfil and to bring God's Holy
Law to the nations and of preserving its exclusiveness and particularity as God's chosen people at all costs. The existence of
a new homeland has greatly strengthened its self-identity, but
this very identity is an obstacle to a true dialogue with other
religions. A majority of Jews does not wish to engage in a

religious dialogue at all. Moreover, the existence of a 'secular'
Jewish state with strong religious overtones points to the fact
that Judaism must reject all claims of a secular ideology.
According to its scriptures, all the nations will one day worship
one and the same God on Mount Zion. Both Islam and
Judaism are further greatly preoccupied in 'putting their own
house in order'. Various conservative and liberal interpretations of their faith continue to threaten the unity of their
religion. Their international organizations serve to assist the
development of the religious, social and cultural life of their
faithful throughout the world and are hardly interested in
approaching other religious or secular institutions.

The cry 'workers of the world unite' died out several decades
ago. Proletarians in several communist countries have become
a new ruling bourgeois class, frequently as much a menace
and an exploitative force in the eyes of the non-white Third
World proletariat as the capitalist strongholds in the West.
Today one must speak of several communist ideologies, each
inspiring peoples in different situations and each claiming to
follow the right Marxist-Leninist strategy for the revolutionary
overthrow of bourgeois society and the birth of an entirely
new and finally human society. But to speak of different
'models' of communism has become a heresy; one can only
follow the one or the other official model which is universally
applicable and valid. The history of the Communist International would perhaps have been less marked by schisms, con-
demnations and excommunications if communist leaders had
studied the story of the Christian church carefully. Communism is split up into several camps which distrust and fight
one another and proselytize as much as the churches in the past.
Hardly any communist community shows an interest in understanding religious phenomena and in keeping close contacts
with religious groups. Much communist ideology is strengthened by pseudo-religious motives and claims to address itself
to the deepest needs and hopes of mankind. Precisely religion,
therefore, remains a principal enemy, undermining man's autonomous and independent efforts to build up a totally secular

society which will replace all previous religious cultures, the Christian civilization in particular.

If we compare the World Council of Churches as one religious group with other world religious groups and secular movements, we must now enquire to what extent the Council considers itself to be a factor in building a true world community of communities, and in what area it has made an authentic and visible contribution to the unity of mankind. At the end of the first chapter I introduced the question whether the World Council understands itself primarily as a community in the midst of and in the service of other communities. I also asked whether in comparison with other international religious and secular organizations the Council has escaped the danger of exclusively serving the needs and interests of its faithful and whether its search for unity in its own ranks is clearly related to the struggle for a world community.

In the course of my presentation of the World Council, its activities and its concerns, I have on occasion mentioned the problem of the Council's self-understanding and identity. According to its Basis, the Council is 'a fellowship of churches which confess the Lord Jesus Christ as God and Saviour and therefore seek to fufil together their common calling'. How are these words to be interpreted in the context of the humanness and humaneness of the Council as a human institution? Discussing the concern for dialogue with people of other living faiths and particularly with other ideologies, we have noticed that the World Council frequently prefers to witness to its faith rather than to listen attentively and patiently to others. Many churches consider dialogue as a threat to or a betrayal of mission. Dialogue is an unsatisfactory means and channel of communication. Referring to the aims and functions of the Council's Unit II, we noted that a major emphasis is placed on 'the mobilization of the whole people of God in the fields of service, development, justice and peace'. The *Christian* responsibility for a world society and the carrying out of that responsibility seems to be the main focus beyond the church's boundaries. The phrase 'therefore seek to fulfil together their common calling' can be interpreted as meaning: seek to find and to affirm their Christian identity. The wider world seems to exist in the first place as an external environment and field of action for the World Council of Churches and its constituent bodies. It is precisely here that the whole problem of the World Council's genuine contribution to humanity as a whole becomes acute. The value of this contribution depends greatly on the Council's critical understanding of the degree of humanness of its own organization and its proper approach to its own human identity as well as Christian identity. In the following three sections we shall see that the World Council has to struggle more consciously and more intensively with these very problems and questions which were less crucial during the first fifteen years of its existence.

'Sacred Literature'

In the year 1959 the well-known Protestant theologian Karl Barth wrote: 'The outlook today would be quite different in some negotiations and conferences if there were at least as honest and open and practical a concern for the reunion of the nations as there has been for the union of the Churches at Edinburgh, Stockholm, Amsterdam, Evanston, etc., and as there is continually in Geneva, not in the Palace of Nations, but in Route de Malagnou 17.'* Route de Malagnou was the old address of the World Council of Churches in the centre of Geneva before it moved out to its much larger and spacious headquarters in the 'international section' of Geneva, close to the United Nations and opposite the World Health Organization and the International Labour Office. One should add that Karl Barth has expressed himself with considerable caution and reserve about the aims and purpose of the ecumenical movement in several of his writings.

The paragraph which I have just quoted still applies to the World Council of Churches today. Over twenty-five years the

* Karl Barth, *Church Dogmatics*, IV, 3, 1, T. & T. Clark, Edinburgh 1961, p. 38.

Council has contributed greatly to the recovery of a more visible and institutional unity of a large number of Christian churches throughout the world. It has been able to bring many Christian communities out of their isolation and to draw them into consultation with one another. Orthodox, Anglican and various Protestant churches, separated for centuries by several barriers, live again as members of a family, 'a family in which there is still a great deal of friction and misunderstanding, but a family which cannot fail to realize that it has a common history and a common destiny'. Even churches living under the pressure of a hostile environment have come into the ecumenical movement. In the World Council and through it the churches still have manifold opportunities to know each other better and to understand each other at deeper levels. Thanks to the Council's clarity of faith, alertness, openness and its international composition, the member churches have frequently rendered a common Christian witness in international conflicts and tensions. The World Council has further enabled its constituent bodies 'to practise solidarity in their relations with each other and to become an effective instrument for the meeting of human need in all parts of the world'.

In the second and third chapter I have referred in outline to the imaginative and untiring efforts of the Council to communicate its various ecumenical concerns to national and local churches, to missionary organizations, to other ecumenical bodies, to laymen and laywomen, to the young generation, through a vast number of studies, publications, consultations, travels, conferences, resolutions and common actions. The fabulous amount of documents, reports, addresses, circular letters, minutes of meetings, consultation digests and records of conferences in the Library of the World Council of Churches testifies to all these endeavours. There is plenty of material for a few dozen more ecumenical doctoral dissertations. In the brief description of the activities of the Council's Programme Unit II, Justice and Service, it has also become clear, I hope, that the World Council has not only been engaged in a world-wide charitable service. Beyond aiding victims of continuous natural or man-made disasters, feeding the hungry, giving care to the sick, providing shelter and re-settlement to refugees, it has facilitated the transfer of re-sources, human and material, for projects and programmes of nation building, development and social welfare. It has mobilized the churches in the world-wide struggle against racism and expressed solidarity in word and deed with the racially oppressed. It has stimulated and assisted Christian participation in the just resolution of international conflicts, pleaded for the protection and implementation of human rights and promoted the spirit of reconciliation in world affairs. All these activities cannot be taken for granted nor should they be minimized.

Yet, many Christians more or less openly today confess that after twenty-five years the World Council of Churches is in an impasse and faces a series of crises. This general feeling has a deeper foundation than most of the various criticisms of the Council to which I referred in the fourth chapter. It is not sufficient, people now admit, to correct some weak parts of the Council's structure and administration, to improve its staff morale and to update its public image. Some new and fundamental questions have to be faced in a world perspective: Who are the World Council? What is the Council really for? What is it that really identifies it within the world community? These very problems have hardly been mentioned and dis-cussed in ecumenical reports and documents. The Council actu-ally renders no good service to itself, to its constituency and to other communities in the world because it hesitates to come openly to grips with the worldly dimensions of its own exis-tence and identity. Thus there is no really adequate human and humanizing network of bi-lateral (inter-church) and multi-lateral (world-wide) communication. Serving the interests and needs of its faithful, the World Council does not seem to be in a position to promote self-analytical and self-critical publi-cations.

One can hardly be surprised, therefore, that much ecumeni-cal literature produced over twenty-five years has a peculiar quality of euphoria and ecumenical equilibrium. A host of

World Council documents deals, sometimes very adequately and pointedly, with all kinds of issues and trends within the church and the world, but they do not really uncover the hidden inner struggles, difficulties and doubts within the World Council of Churches itself. Has not the Council, after all, a solid christocentric Basis, which, even if it is not a creed or a confession of faith, serves as a safe guideline for the churches' common witness and their common action? Thus what is written in numerous reports about the World Council itself is to be accepted as the 'normative' and 'authentic' literature which can be worthy of praise but does not deserve blame. If the churches loyally 'study and implement' the recommendations of the World Council as to how to witness, to serve and to be involved in the life of the world, they will continue to grow together and the full purpose of the ecumenical movement will eventually be realized.

Much ecumenical literature is indeed infected with some kind of idolatry. The ecumenical movement itself is frequently approached as a 'sacred cow' which has to be fed and cannot be touched because of certain ecumenical taboos. I must confess that in the process of writing this book I too have become guilty of having adapted myself too quickly to a smooth ecumenical jargon. I have described the functions and activities of some World Council sub-units in a typically ecumenical (euphemistic) fashion. My short and generous revaluation of the World Council of Churches in the light of Karl Barth's praise of the Council is another example of glossing over ecumenical issues and not getting down to the roots of some real problems with many human dimensions and implications, which are part of the World Council of Churches' very being.

An institution like the World Council is, of course, in no way unique in being trapped in its official and consensus-building language and having great difficulty in communicating in more human ways with its constituency and external environment. Several current sociological studies show that all institutions, whether secular or religious, suffer from identity crises, erect clever façades by producing a host of intelligently conceived propagandistic literature which seemingly inspires even 'sophisticated' followers, and avoid noticing pressures and disturbances which hint at the necessity for a radical change in their institutional behaviour. Any institution is too much occupied with itself and its proper self-expression. Insisting on being itself, it has little interest in developing a more profound communication with other institutions and contributing to an understanding of a truly human interdependence of other institutions and communities. Imposing its living and working patterns on others, it must pretend in its publications and records that it is moving on its own in the right direction and outside the reach of any fundamental criticism. Thus its communication is often conducted in dehumanizing ways. As the survival of the institution is at stake, an outward-looking response to its being called in question cannot be considered as a renewal but only as the undermining of its very existence. This sociological analysis of institutional life and behaviour cannot be used, however, as an excuse for the World Council's timid and inadequate attempt to face its predicament squarely and to refer in articulate ways to the difficult situation in which it operates. The problems of true identity and change, of becoming and of being more human, should concern Christians at least as much as others. Unless ecumenical literature becomes less official, less well-balanced and less 'sacred', the presence of the World Council of Churches in the world community of communities and its role and function *vis-à-vis* other international organizations and movements will remain ambiguous and unclear. Unless a greater self-criticism (the Christian equivalent of this term is 'repentance') is exercised and a greater modesty (self-denial) is explicitly manifested, the Council's credibility as a *Christian* world organization with a *world* purpose will not increase.

Salt and Leaven

In a recent article, entitled 'Man's Inhumanity to Man', Canon David Jenkins, Director of the World Council's *Humanum* Studies, points to the unsatisfactory and problematic nature of

the Council's response to the world in which it has to live and
be true to its aims. In fact he calls the very identity and
activities of the World Council in question and comes to a
similar conclusion that the surrounding world constitutes the
external environment of the World Council of Churches and
its constituency. 'It is not the world which produces the
agenda,' he writes. 'It is, in fact, the tremors which the world's
agenda sets up within the institution, and which are then
transformed into the institution's concerns, which produce
the actual agendas that are worked on. These agendas, of
course, are mostly sterile as far as the world is concerned, for
the world has not actually been listened to, only reacted to.'
He continues: 'Failure to listen in time and respond in time
will result either in the complete sealing off of the institution
which may survive for a remarkably long time in an irrelevant
limbo of obsolescence or else in the institution's breaking up.
The latter fate has more saving possibilities than the former.
Presumably we can rely on the mercy of God to ensure that
the irrelevancies of ecclesiastical organizations are not too
tough.'*

The World Council of Churches has indeed reached a critical
stage, as it seems not to be sufficiently aware of the necessity
of developing a critical self-awareness and of putting its Christian identity at risk. The unconsciousness of a potential inhumanity of the very structures in which it operates can
indeed lead to a sealing off of its fate. The Council's predicament is even more serious when it consciously tries to safe-
guard its very identity, but in the wrong way and at the
wrong end. Preparing for the Commission meeting in Louvain
in 1972, the Sub-Unit on Faith and Order published a study
document entitled *The Unity of the Church and the Unity
of Mankind*. The unity of the church is throughout the study
primarily considered in the context of Christian identity. The
document refers to an 'uncertainty of the Churches as to
whether positive international action is a fulfilment of their

* David E. Jenkins, 'Man's Inhumanity to Man', *Ecumenical Review* XXV,
1, January 1973, p. 17.

mission or anti-Christian self-assertion'. It further expresses
great fear that the church assuming its role in the secular
world will lose its identity and character as salt and leaven,
being 'swallowed up by an all-pervasive humanism'.

There are apparently different interpretations of the two
New Testament parables of the church as leaven and salt. It
does not seem to be understood that it is the function of the
leaven to make the firm, heavy and indigestible dough turn
into light and digestible bread. When the bread is finally baked,
the leaven has lost its own substance. The same is true for the
durableness and the flavour of salt. It is not the task of the
church to make the entire world salty, but to enrich many
human beings with greater solidity and vigilance facing the
complicated problems and staggering tasks of this world. The
salt enables men not to grow weak or to despair, but to hope
for an open future and a fulfilment of all things. As the leaven
has to disappear in the bread, the salt must be consumed in
the food, in order that the produced effect can be noticed. In
contrast to the leaven, the salt has a preserving function. Once
it has lost its savour, however, it can neither salt the food nor
preserve it. The church is not in danger of losing its 'task' by
pervading the world; the risk lies in its becoming a 'tasteless'
community. If that happens the salt can be thrown away.

The two parables yield another lesson. Neither the flour
nor the food are bad and unfit for consumption. On the contrary, they are both destined to be nourishment for human
beings. Only their substance and flavour are improved when
leaven or salt are added. The Faith and Order document is,
therefore, on a wrong track in raising the question whether
in its contacts with the world the church will be secularized
and lose its Christian identity. If reference is made to a twofold danger that the church 'may lose itself in the world and
therefore lose the source of true community', or else, that 'it
may become a static community and therefore cease to be a
community builder', the discussion on possible relationships
between the church and the world starts from the wrong side.
A similar mistake is made when it is pretended that there is a

problematic tension between 'the priestly mission of reconciliation among men, and the prophetic mission of rebuking
evil and making militant cause against its attacks upon God's
creatures and upon the People of God in particular'. All these
and other difficult alternative choices are formulated in order
that the church can continue to claim the distinctiveness of
its boundaries and the sacredness of its calling as a community
on its own. This is indeed an un-Christian and wrong defence
of the church's identity.

When the ecumenical church is from the outset deeply
identified with the world in its aspirations, its achievements,
its restlessness and its despair – when the leaven is penetrating
the bread and the salt the food – it has no need to worry either
about the meaning and content of its priestly mission of reconciliation among men or about the right understanding of itself
as a particular, provisional community. Being at the same time
a *human* community and a peculiar people of God, the church
at every moment and at every place loses itself in binding up
wounds, caused by aggression, hate, prejudice and greed, by
'sticking out its neck' in the battle for more just political and
socio-economic structures, and by serving whole-heartedly the
provisional goal of a greater humanization of an international
society. In particular, its continuous *being* in open communication with peoples adhering to another faith or ideology and
its *public* affirmation that in many dialogues it can learn
'lessons for life' from others, can make the church humble and
admit that it cannot be a 'glorious' but isolated community
on its own.

Only if the church exercises all this gladly but also 'in the
sweat of its brow' for the sake of the unity of mankind, will
the danger of its turning more into a static, sterile and sub-
human community be overcome and will moments of a
critical, prophetic and even militant mission arrive. The warning words of the 'watchman', such as: the achievement of an
universal cosmopolitan state must be regarded as unrealistic
and illusory; hope in the kingdom of God permits only complete devotion to certain limited goals; man can be the creator

of a more human world, but also his own 'grave-digger'; the
world is deserted by God and mortally dangerous, but also
'basically habitable'; etc., are then called for and can be very
much to the point. I will come back to this prophetic function
of the World Council and the churches it represents in a
moment.

The Disunity of the Church

It seems that the Faith and Order theme 'The Unity of the
Church and the Unity of Mankind' just mentioned could also
be formulated with the phrase: 'The Disunity of the Church
and the Unity of Mankind'. There is neither irony nor male-
volence in this proposal. The point is that the church needs to
be set free from its ecclesiastical alienation and its false Christian identity in the interest of a greater unity of mankind. The
church and the World Council of Churches should know that
an international Christian communion cannot be based on
pious intentions and eirenic principles. The church has
received its life and is nurtured by the cross and the resurrection of its Lord and Saviour, Jesus Christ. His cross is the very
basis and condition of any Christian community. His suffering,
his defeat, his death and his resurrection are the *raison d'être*
of the World Council of Churches. It is the Lord who addresses
the words to the Council and its constituency: 'If anyone
wishes to be a follower of mine, he must leave self behind;
day after day he must take up his cross, and come with me.
Whoever cares for his own safety is lost; but if a man will let
himself be lost for my sake, that man is safe. What will a man
gain by winning the whole world, at the cost of his true self?'
(Luke 9.23-25).

These words imply that there is conflict, confrontation, controversy and polarization in the Christian community. There
is weakness, disillusionment and defeat in the World Council
of Churches. Being involved in the ecumenical movement
means fighting together, repenting together, growing together,
changing together. No one is spared taking up his cross; the
experience of falling down and standing up must come to each

church. The cross itself is the supreme clue to the understanding of the precarious and delicate condition of the Christian community, of any human community and the world
community of communities. Only through the cross of Jesus
Christ can a community become more human and will the
unity of mankind not remain an utter utopia. It is, therefore,
no shame to speak of the disunity and, to use even a stronger
word, of the disintegration of the church. Only what is lost
can be saved. The institution which tries to save itself by claiming that it has an indestructible identity is lost. Bearing its daily
cross, the World Council can put its identity at risk and regain
its authentic identity in its Master, Jesus Christ, the Lord of
all human history. Christian institutional identity will be
restored over and over again when the sinful nature of institutional structures and practices is recognized, and in and
through the cross of its Lord new opportunities 'for endless
identifying with new and renewing ways of being human' are
discovered. Precisely the process of being involved in repentance, change and redirection will enable the Council not to
pretend that it has a more protected identity than other
communities and that, due to its greater unity, it is more in the
forefront facing the world's problems than other institutions.

The disunity of the church continues to baffle the World
Council and to absorb much of its strength. It has been stated
over and over again that no new organization, but only
renewal and rebirth of the actual churches, can lead to a more
authentic and viable world Christian community in true dialogue with the secular world. But so far, more isolated Christian communities are brought into a large isolated Christian
community, and it is not sufficiently seen that by adding up
all the confessional and denominational identities one does not
arrive at the total sum of true Christian identity. Surely one
cannot maintain that the World Council of Churches is a self-
contained international organization. The Council is quite
aware of the fact that all its humanitarian and social operations are but a drop in the ocean of world-wide need. It also
knows that many interventions and efforts at mediation and

reconciliation in world conflicts cannot become immediately apparent. Yet, there are several indications that the churches are satisfied with internationally co-ordinated programmes for development, rescue from hunger, poverty or disaster, the combat of racism, the defence of human rights, the administering of adequate medical services. All this can proclaim their engagement in the world and make up for their own renewal and their delicate search for a true identity which is not obtained by carrying out all these programmes but by *being* the people of God in the midst of *his* world. It is, therefore, no accident that very new and disturbing questions about the humanness and the humanization of the World Council and its constituency are being raised. If the church cannot admit that it suffers from a false identity and that it must continuously struggle to discover the Christian insights for living humanly, which means listening first of all to the world and not using the world as a field of operation, it indeed contributes little to the world community.

These three points bring us back to other questions which I raised at the end of the introductory chapter. I asked the question whether the World Council of Churches is better prepared to formulate more precisely the concepts of 'humanity' and 'mankind'. In the light of several observations and remarks it has become clear, I hope, that the Council can try to say honestly and humbly that it has only started to wrestle with the problems of how to formulate the unity of the church and the unity of mankind. The Council has reached no agreement about the precise christological point from which it should start or the methodology which it should follow, nor does it know the outcome of further theological reflection on a growing world community. It can only operate with 'open' models of the concept of unity and beware of introducing and imposing notions of unity which would put both the world and the church in a theological or ideological strait-jacket. The dogmatization of particular concepts of unity will only seal off the historical process which carries in itself a more human, more pluralistic and more complex unity. The World Council can grasp anew that the unity of mankind required by God will only be aspired at by participating fully in the actual process of history through experiences of crises and judgments and by dedicating itself to deeper renewal.

How far can the ecumenical movement take the challenge and thrust of certain contemporary ideological movements into account? We have seen that the World Council has not clarified the concept of ideology and is still confused about the ideological presuppositions and implications of its various activities. The whole issue of the relationship between theology and ideology has hardly been touched upon. Yet an increasing number of ecumenical Christians see very clearly that theology, like ideology, is always in danger of playing the role of a competitor. For this reason they have also become sceptical when in the Council and its constituent churches terms such as a 'theology of liberation', a 'theology of revolution', a 'theology of development' are used. They have the feeling that updating theology by adding a number of qualifying nouns comes close to preserving the relevance of ecumenical theology at all costs. In so doing the church seems to keep up with history and to deal critically with man's ambiguous efforts to build up the city of God, but does not realize that by pleading God's cause it has taken his place and has deprived the gospel of its savour, its risk and its promise. It forgets that the Christian faith is not a faith in an idea, nor in what is behind reality, but in God's dealing with history. In analysing a political or ideological situation 'in the light of the gospel', i.e. from its own transcendental point of view, the church ends up hovering above the political and ideological conflicts. By seemingly transcending its own ideological commitments, it has modified theology to a dangerous *status quo* ideology which serves to defend the church's own existence.

Precisely for this reason the World Council of Churches, both for its own sake and in rendering an advisory service to the churches, need not engage hurriedly in its task of defining the role of theology *vis-à-vis* ideology, of separating (artificially) the one from the other, or of introducing the corrective and transcendental elements of faith into the ideological struggle. It is not in spite of but because of God's incarnation in Jesus Christ that the ecumenical movement is going through a period of ideological dynamism with its challenge and testing. The World Council can start to compare its ideological allegiances and positions. There is a clear indication that serious ideological debates can take place on the basis of common Christian commitment and as expression of mutual concern and support.

Questions about the purpose of dialogue with people who hold to certain ideologies, the methods of approach to this dialogue and the specific issues that are at stake will then arise naturally and not artificially out of these difficult but promising exercises. The Council could even eventually suggest that a theme such as 'ideology as a secular faith' is an important subject for discussion, not because it has not fallen in the trap of idolatry, not because it always has recourse to a healing faith, but precisely because it does not always use ideology exclusively as a tool for analysing and understanding the social process. Perhaps it will then have somewhat less difficulty, as has been suggested, in coming into contact not only with more Eastern European Marxists but equally with communists from various countries in the Third World and in inviting them to participate in a new and genuine dialogue. Once better relations are established, new light will be shed on 'the task of clarifying the meaning of the gospel in contexts where Christian faith and ideologies tend to be mixed up, leading to theological confusion and ethical impotence', because the solving of these 'complicated' theological problems does not take place in the realm of intellectual and uncommitted theological reflection, but in the very context of ideological dialogue and daily ideological struggle, which are directed and constantly corrected by the Council's faith in Jesus Christ. Everything depends on whether that faith is truly alive.

I refer once more to the question whether the World Council's entire charitable and social programme is not characterized by a human, sometimes all too human, desire to affirm its Christian identity and to show that it stands in the forefront of the battle against misery, exploitation and socio-economic injustice. I have asked before whether its progressive stand in matters of development, aid to under-developed countries, racial justice, support of liberation movements, human rights, refugees and medical service could not be considered as an inconclusive step beyond its struggle for a deeper manifest-ation of its own unity and beyond its slow progress in common theological reflections. The Council has surely no other choice than to continue 'to pick up the victims that fall by the way' and at the same time to be in the vanguard facing and pene-trating into the manifold problems of national and inter-national human affairs. As man's injustice to man and nations' injustice to nations do not diminish, collective charitable action is called for, and endeavours to facilitate the sharing of material and human resources in a more equal and just way must be made. But where can the line be drawn between a generous activism and a retreat into a subtle self-satisfaction and a comfortable pietism? Or to phrase the question differ-ently : How can the World Council make clear that it does not misuse the world as a field of action and is not afraid to be swallowed up by an all-pervasive humanism?

The Council, to be sure, has constantly to make world-wide appeals and to encourage the churches to subscribe to its various humanitarian and social programmes. It needs to speak directly to the compassion and conscience of many Christians, whatever their creed or confession. But, on the other hand, local and world-wide publicity can easily be interpreted to mean only that the churches have closed their ranks to come to the rescue of thousands of victims of natural or man-made disasters. The impression is created – I have just spoken of the difficulty of reading carefully between the lines of much ecumenical literature – that it is a specific Christian virtue to be concerned with the destiny of many a neighbour near by or far away. The World Council thus represents an inter-national Christian community which is better equipped to deal with human and humanitarian problems than other commun-ities. By its very nature, it cannot be satisfactorily ranged

among other religious or secular institutions and agencies.
The situation becomes even worse when within the World
Council and its constituency it is claimed that the world's
agenda seems to serve only to set up the Council's agenda, to
be transformed into its institutional concerns.

The uneasiness and uncertainty about the meaning and
effect of its service can only be overcome if the Council does
not worry each time about the theological significance and the
specific Christian value of its large Unit II Programme. The
correct reading of the two parables of the church as leaven
and salt is of great importance to the churches' understanding
of their mission. Both leaven and salt are of no specific use in
themselves. They have only performed their function if they
penetrate into and disappear in the bread and the food. That
process is invisible and uncontrollable. This means that Christians simply share intensively the burdens and the hopes of
this world. They are marked by a deep solidarity and true
identification with the human race. Only as Christians engage
in the actual process of advancing together with all men
towards a creative, healthier and stronger world community, is
it permissible for them to speak of human sin and the solidarity
of guilt. Only then can their message of God's forgiveness of
sin and the overcoming of evil in Jesus Christ – the very basis
of all their social and humanitarian actions – become credible
and relevant. Only then is their particular Christian identity
again and again given to them. And perhaps then it may dawn
upon secular and other religious men alike that the crucified
and risen Christ continues to hold this globe together in one
single unity.

VIII

The Promise of a World Community

Some fellow-Christians, having read the preceding pages, could object that my enquiry in this book, namely whether the World Council of Churches has made a contribution of its own to a new world community, including all mankind, has been based on sound biblical exegesis and valid theological principals. The impression has been created, they may protest, that a genuine, peaceful and just community of mankind will be attained in any circumstances and that the World Council has to perform a specific Christian role in the process of developing a viable world community. Consequently it may seem that, although I criticized the universal brotherhood movements of this century and their aims and goals severely in the opening chapter, I myself have written in too optimistic, evolutionary and non-theological terms about the possibility of realizing, before or after the year 2000, a world society at peace, under common law and order and united in one brotherhood of the human race.

I wish to reply that I had no intention of concealing in any way the deep polarities and conflicts which are tearing the present international society asunder. As a Christian, I am deeply aware of the fact that sinful tendencies in the midst of mankind persistently seek to violate the hope and goal of a world community. The unity of mankind is still an ambiguous concept, and the march towards the unity of the human race should be described more frequently in terms of disagreement, tension and clash than in terms of understanding, harmony and peace. It does indeed remain a very open question whether men will ever live together in greater accord and solidarity, because all human beings are sinful and plagued by the perplexity of the problem of individual and corporate evil. As much as it is true that no man, group or nation can live for himself or itself, individuals and human communities are constantly threatened by a parochialism in all thinking and a sectarian 'over-against-ness'. The one interdependent world in which we now live creates as many new freedoms and new forms of wider community as new conflicts, new exploitations and divisions. At the present stage of world history we know all too well that the progressive spread of scientific and technological civilization is producing new forms of human separation, bondage and manipulation. As I said at the outset of this book, the unifying impact of technology and science does not automatically imply the development towards a more just, harmonious and meaningful society and communal human relationships at a deeper level. On the contrary, for the first time in human history, mankind is threatened with a universal self-destruction.

Thus the World Council and its member churches, in being faithful to their mission and fulfilling their task, have to live in tension and disagreement with the divided and often unsuccessful secular world. They cannot be sure whether positive international action is a fulfilment of their mission or anti-Christian self-assertion. Assuming its role of mediation and reconciliation, but also of prophetic warning in the midst of dangerous and frustrating world affairs, the church must be concerned not to become worldly itself, and thereby to lose its own identity and character as leaven and salt in this world. The achievement of a community of all mankind in all its variety of colour, culture and creed, cannot be its foremost goal. Its primary task remains the proclamation of the all-transcending hope of the kingdom of God.

The ecumenical movement can and should indeed be characterized by the daily and firm faith that the kingdom of God is the only answer to man's quest for a world community. At the World Council's First Assembly at Amsterdam in 1948 it was already emphasized in the official message that 'the final judgment on all human history and on every human deed is the judgment of the merciful Christ; and that the end of history will be the triumph of His Kingdom, where alone we shall understand how much God has loved the world'. The unlimited reign of God over this world is the future and hope of the Christian church and the world. In God's kingdom man will find his completion and fulfilment. This kingdom is at the same time the kingdom of man, 'his new heaven and his new earth'. In this kingdom of God also (and not before), the unity of the church and the unity of mankind will not only coincide fully but be transformed in the one and single unity between God and men. In other words, there will be only one world community and no longer a world community of communities under God's eternal reign.

On the way to this one unity of mankind in God, the church represents humanity, and as an institutional entity is but an instrument for the attainment of that goal. The unity of the church should never become a unity in itself, as the church just as much as mankind and together with mankind is moving towards the coming ultimate reign of God. Since salvation in Christ is offered to the entire world, it is not up to Christians to draw a demarcation line between the church and the multi-religious and secular world. God himself and alone distinguishes the boundary line in mankind. Christians, therefore, cannot differentiate between believers, other-believers and non-believers in the way men and women are placed in separate categories. Within the church and within mankind one and the same human being for whom Christ died and was raised from the dead is called before God.

Proclaiming the kingdom of God in our ecumenical era, the church must beware not to repeat the errors of nineteenth- and early twentieth-century liberal theology in using the term 'kingdom of God' in connection with the principles of the

Enlightenment and explaining the reign of God as the fellowship of moral endeavour founded by Jesus Christ. The notion
that men, united in love, can exercise their lordship over the
world by their work in life and help each other to perfection
has been corrected by the eschatological notion that God's
kingdom can never be accomplished within the confines of
history because of human limitations. It is only 'the gratuitous-
ness, and incalculability of God's grace' and the comprehen-
siveness of his bestowal of salvation, which takes in the whole
of the world and history into his kingdom. This implies that the
consummation of all things in God is far more than the establishment of a world-wide responsible society, the end of
hunger, oppression and exploitation. The 'abundant life' in his
kingdom includes the abolition of death and man's eternal
communion with his Creator.

Yet, it also remains true that Christians and their fellow
human beings share effectively in the building of God's kingdom if their efforts aim at the establishment of a world which
is unified in peace, justice and joy. If man's false security in
the old and his fear for revolutionary change tempt him to
defend the *status quo* or to patch it up with half-hearted
measures, he may well perish. Because of their faith in the
coming kingdom of God and in their search for his righteous-
ness, Christians cannot but participate in the continuous
struggle of millions of people for greater socio-economic
justice, for world development and a global community. The
church's deep involvement in, and identification with, the
world's ideological battles and their new openness to families
of other living faiths for the sake of a more unified world
is directly and intimately related to the coming of the
kingdom.

The World Council of Churches' task of recognizing itself
fully and acting as one world community in the midst of and
for the sake of other world communities is a humble, precarious and promising one. Its witness to the all-transcending
kingdom of God should be accompanied by its confession that
the church has been sectional in its views of itself as over

against the world. Much of its theological reflection has often
centred in 'the people of God', as if the rest of mankind were
not also God's people. A denial of community is a denial of the
humanity of the other. Giving account of the vision in Christ of
a world society, the World Council and its churches cannot
afford to gloss over the gulf between the vision and the actu-
ality in the life of the church. Not only the world but also the
church has not known the community to which it testifies.
Only in great humility can the church speak of itself 'as the
sign of the coming unity of mankind'. Although it is true that
Jesus Christ gathers together the nucleus of a new community
as the first fruits of a new mankind, the church at various
occasions is and must be perplexed about the divisions in its
own ranks, the frequent cheapness of its concepts like 'reconciliation', 'hope' and 'love', and its underestimation of costly
Christian partisanship with the forgotten and down-trodden
of the earth.

For these very reasons, the World Council of Churches, as
a hopeful and struggling world community, needs to meet the
world communities of Islam and Judaism. They also have a
message of the ultimate destiny of mankind. The prophet
Jeremiah proclaims a new covenant by which men's hearts will
be changed. The prophets Isaiah and Micah describe the new
reign of Yahweh as unmixed happiness which is imparted
through Israel to all the nations and will bring about an inward
transformation, taking in the whole earth and indeed the whole
creation. This promise of salvation also includes doing away
with death. The Qur'ān teaches that while the rewards and
joys experienced in the life after death will be everlasting and
ever-intensifying, the pains and torments will come to an end;
all mankind will ultimately find admission to the grace and
mercy of God. 'Allah is well pleased with them and they are
well pleased with him.' Both Judaism and Islam, however, also
share with Christianity the perplexities of being divided in
their respective communities and not living and expressing
from the depth of their hearts their ultimate hope.

Bearing the stigmata of Western civilization, of a Western

philosophy of history and progress, and of Western belief in the scientific and technological mastering of this world, the World Council of Churches also needs to come into much deeper contact with the Asian religions of Hinduism and Buddhism. Salvation in history and the kingdom of God, as I indicated before, are strange and unknown concepts to these religions. Their search for the meaning of life goes above and beyond the limits of any particular human community and world history. Man cannot discover himself within the process of history; it is his historically conditioned being which must be overcome and transcended. Man must be attuned to the Spirit in continuous worship and silence, penetrating into the depth of his soul, which reaches salvation only after a long process of utter self-denial and ceaseless purification. Western man judges these exercises for life too mystical, too unproductive and time-consuming. Religion, according to him, must meet his immediate needs and assure him a meaningful place in a purposeful history. Christians accustomed to being active in one way or another, to organizing and building a religious community and to drawing other people into that well-defined community, can learn something from Hinduism and Buddhism, which 'lack' a unified ecclesiastical organization. Interfaith dialogue at the level of the Spirit can throw a searching and disturbing light on the false securities of Christians, on the real reasons for their attachments and convictions, on their desire through shallow religious attitudes to compensate for inadequacies they dare not face and on the self-expression of their egos, which too easily they pass off as desire for the conversion of others. The Asian faiths add a whole other dimension to the quest of a world community of communities. Precisely because Asians cannot think or speak of a kingdom of God as the ultimate fulfilment of history, the Christian ecumenical movement must be at considerable pain and anguish not to claim for itself the fullness of divine revelation and to deliver self-confidently and in Western conquering style the message of God's reign over all humanity. The coming of the kingdom does not depend on man's deepest desire for community and his most noble involvement extending that community.

On the other hand, the Council and its world-wide constituency should without hesitation acknowledge that secular ideologies are not unrelated to the kingdom of God. The communist will and passion to build with all human strength and with all available means a radically different and new society frequently exceed the Christian commitment to promote a more just and more human community. Among various communist endeavours particular mention should be made of the recent gigantic Chinese enterprise of trying to solve a number of seemingly unsolvable domestic problems accumulated over many centuries by enlisting the world's largest community in one common national responsibility and mutual service to the people. The church is on a wrong track when it condemns Marxist-Leninist ideology exclusively on the grounds of its atheist principles. There can never be a genuine Christian front against atheism. The church must abandon all false alliances formed in order to oppose communist atheism. Communism is first of all to be criticized for its social utopianism. It gravely underestimates the power of evil and the human will-to-power. Although Marxism deviates from universal brotherhood movements and liberal Christianity by interpreting history as a process of inevitable and catastrophic class struggle, it nevertheless projects the 'kingdom of God' as an immanent force in history, culminating in a universal society of justice, harmony and peace. It is caught in the inner conflict of defining itself as a rational, historic form of thought based on empiricism, and its messianic claim to absolutism. As it does not take man's true nature sufficiently into account, it has great difficulty in changing its abstract humanism into a concrete humanism.

The Christian faith does not condemn communist ideology 'for being too materialistic, but for being too idealistic, not for being too rationalistic but for not being rational enough'. Human life and human society will never be free from exploitations, perplexities and problems. Arguing with Marxism-Leninism in this way, the church may contribute to a communist break-away from atheism – both in its dogmatic metaphysical and in its practical form – which indeed nourishes the idea of historical self-redemption and the romantic sentiment of universal proletarian comradeship. Still, Christians engaged in a Marxist-Christian dialogue around the world are in danger of speaking glibly of God's intervention in history and of his plan of salvation beyond human reach. Jesus' parable of the pounds makes it quite clear that those who have been faithful in a little will receive more. The communist's stress on man's utter responsibility for this one and only life may bring him nearer to the kingdom of God than the Christian who has put his pound away awaiting the return of his Master. The ecumenical movement, in facing various communist communities, should be more joyfully aware of this fact.

The churches' task of recognizing themselves fully and acting as the Christian world community in the midst of and for the sake of other world communities is again a humble, precarious and promising one, when the eucharist is celebrated throughout this world. Christians rightly confess that participation in the eucharist and incorporation in the death and resurrection of Christ is not only the sole foundation of the church's universal fellowship but also the pre-eminent manifestation and anticipation of the ultimate unity of mankind. In the eucharist Christians experience with their total being the true liberation from all bondage and their reception into lasting and indissoluble communion. But even armed with a 'eucharist-centred eschatology', Christians cannot struggle against both ecclesiastical triumphalism and secular utopianism, unless they 'hurry back' to the battlefields of this divided world and convince others that contemporary efforts towards building a wider community, both on the local and the world level, can be regarded as participation in *God's* action.

The World Council of Churches is a factor in building world community as it wrestles within itself and in the midst of this world with the living God and struggles to be open for wider community. It is that factor when it speaks honestly and modestly of the visible and invisible unity of the church –

when will all Christians celebrate the eucharist together ? – but honestly and boldly of its share in the burdens and hopes of this world. It is that factor as it searches for a new quality of community – local and world-wide – and does not forget to express that not only is humanity extremely broken but Christians everywhere suffer from each other and cause suffering to each other. It is that factor when it prays for the unexpected and explosive working of the Spirit and at the same time tries to break through the many barriers of communication with other world organizations and movements. It is that factor when it tests its credibility in the world and discovers at the same time that its very own identity is not endangered or stifled but deepened and promoted. It is that factor as it asks for God's forgiveness for frequently obscuring more than manifesting the coming of his kingdom, the one and only hope of mankind.

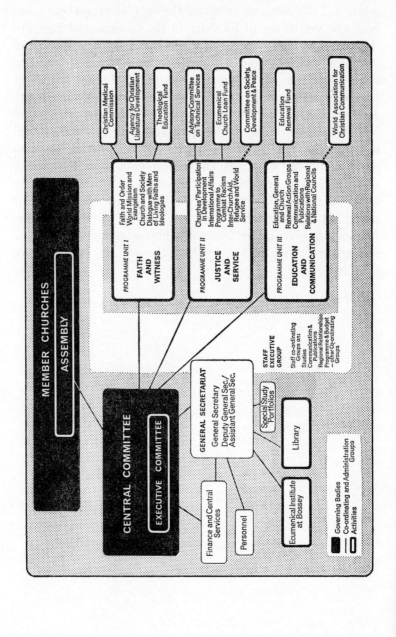

MEMBER CHURCHES

ASSEMBLY

CENTRAL COMMITTEE

EXECUTIVE COMMITTEE

GENERAL SECRETARIAT
General Secretary
Deputy General Sec./
Assistant General Sec.

Finance and Central Services

Personnel

Special Study Portfolios

Library

Ecumenical Institute at Bossey

STAFF EXECUTIVE GROUP
Staff co-ordinating Groups on:
Studies
Communication &
Publications
Regional Relationships
— Programme & Budget
— other Co-ordinating Groups

PROGRAMME UNIT I
FAITH AND WITNESS
Faith and Order
World Mission and Evangelism
Church and Society
Dialogue with Men of Living Faiths and Ideologies

PROGRAMME UNIT II
JUSTICE AND SERVICE
Churches' Participation in Development
Commission of the Churches on International Affairs
Programme to Combat Racism
Inter-Church Aid, Refugee and World Service

PROGRAMME UNIT III
EDUCATION AND COMMUNICATION
Education, General and Church
Renewal Action Groups
Communication and Publications
Relations with Regional & National Councils

Christian Medical Commission
Agency for Christian Literature Development
Theological Education Fund

Advisory Committee on Technical Services
Ecumenical Church Loan Fund
Committee on Society, Development & Peace

Education Renewal Fund

World Association for Christian Communication

Governing Bodies
Co-ordinating and Administration Groups
Activities

FOR FURTHER READING

DICKINSON, RICHARD, *Line and Plummet. The Churches and Development*, Geneva: World Council of Churches 1968, 112 pp.

A reflection on the role of Christian churches in socio-economic development of the less-developed countries, to stimulate discussion and action.

FEY, HAROLD E. (ed.), *The Ecumenical Advance. A History of the Ecumenical Movement, Volume 2, 1948-1968*, London: SPCK 1970, 524 pp.

The 'official' history of the ecumenical movement and the World Council of Churches since its founding in 1948. Contains various contributions by World Council staff members and ecumenical theologians. A detailed and comprehensive bibliography of ecumenical literature is added.

GOODALL, NORMAN, *Ecumenical Progress. A Decade of Change in the Ecumenical Movement, 1961-71*, London: Oxford University Press 1972, 173 pp.

A sequel to his book *The Ecumenical Movement: What it is and what it does* (1964). Brings together information not accessible in many other volumes. The author has been long associated with the World Council in several different capacities.

JENKINS, DAVID, 'Man's Inhumanity to Man. The Direction and Purpose of the Humanum Studies', *Ecumenical Review* XXV, no. 1, Jan. 1973, pp. 5-28.

The thesis of this important article is that the World Council of Churches and its constituent bodies 'need to learn and practice administrative and institutional repentance – which involves a great deal of personal and individual repentance'.

NOLDE, O. FREDERICK, *The Churches and the Nations*, Philadelphia: Fortress Press 1970, 184 pp.

Dr Nolde was from the very beginning in 1946 Director of the World Council's Commission of the Churches on International Affairs. His book records the contribution of the churches to world politics and shows how Christians, individually and collectively, can take increasing responsibility in the quest for world peace, justice and harmony.

SAMARTHA, STANLEY J., *Living Faiths and the Ecumenical Movement*, Geneva: World Council of Churches 1971, 182 pp.
A collection of papers representing the discussion among Christians about the nature of the enterprise of dialogue with many living faiths, and about the understandings of Christian faith and mission that are appropriate.

TILL, BARRY, *The Churches Search for Unity*, Harmondsworth: Penguin Books 1972, 556 pp.
A brief but comprehensive survey of the ecumenical movement, past and present. Starting from the teachings of the New Testament it records recent and current efforts of the World Council of Churches and other bodies, and closely examines the attitudes adopted by the Roman Catholic and Orthodox Churches to the question of unity. Religious differences can only truly be resolved at 'grass-roots' level. The World Council is rather critically approached.

VINCENT, JOHN, *The Race Race*, London: SCM Press 1970, 116 pp.
An ecumenical report on the Consultation on Race in Notting Hill, London, under the auspices of the World Council in 1969. Shows how racialism today has developed, pictures what it is like to be on the receiving end of racial oppression, and gives some indication of what the churches have and have not done to combat it.

VISSER 'T HOOFT, WILLEM ADOLF, *Memoirs*, London: SCM Press 1973, 379 pp.
The author was the first General Secretary of the World Council of Churches, from its foundation until his retirement in 1966. His memoirs give an account of the experience of a man who has been involved in international ecumenical life for more than fifty years.

WARD, MARCUS, *The Churches Move Together*, Nutfield, Surrey: Denholm House Press 1968, 102 pp.
An account, in compact form, of the ecumenical movement from the Edinburgh Conference of 1910 and its impact on the churches in Great Britain. Convinced of the need for unity Dr Ward reports what has been achieved and what still remains to be done.